Table Of Contents

Section 6: Advanced Techniques for Power Users

Section 7: Troubleshooting and Optimization

Section 8: Real-World Use Cases

Section 9: Scaling and Future-Proofing

Conclusion

- Recap: Key Takeaways for Success
- Next Steps for Continuous Improvement

Appendices

- **Appendix A:** Glossary of Key Terms
- **Appendix B:** Recommended Plugins and Extensions
- **Appendix C:** Further Reading and Resources

Disclaimer

This book is an independent resource and is not officially affiliated with, endorsed by, or sponsored by any company, organization, or trademark holder referenced within. All trademarks, service marks, product names, and company names or logos mentioned are the property of their respective owners. Use of these names or terms is solely for identification and reference purposes, and no association or endorsement by the respective trademark holder is implied. The content of this book is based on publicly available information, the author's research, and personal insights. This book is intended for educational and informational purposes only.

Introduction

The Power of Seamless Collaboration in Modern Project Management

Introduction to Seamless Collaboration

In today's fast-paced, innovation-driven business landscape, project management is no longer just about deadlines and task lists—it's about *collaboration*. Teams are increasingly cross-functional, distributed, and working on complex deliverables that require constant synchronization. Without effective collaboration, even the most well-planned projects can derail. Seamless collaboration isn't a buzzword—it's the bedrock of success in modern project management.

The Shift Toward Integrated Workflows

Gone are the days when email threads and static documents could serve as the central nervous system of a project. Modern teams require real-time communication, centralized information sharing, and tools that adapt to their workflow—not the other way around. This has led to a growing demand for integrated digital ecosystems that break down silos, reduce friction, and provide a unified space for planning, execution, and review.

Seamless collaboration means every team member has access to the same source of truth, is aware of ongoing updates, and can contribute in ways that add immediate value—without needing to switch between disjointed tools or repeat manual processes.

Why Collaboration Matters More Than Ever

The complexity of projects has increased with digital transformation, remote work, and global operations. Modern projects often involve:

- Multiple stakeholders with differing objectives
- Agile methodologies that require iterative coordination
- High volumes of information and documentation
- Rapid change and continuous delivery

Without seamless collaboration, these elements become liabilities. Information gaps, misaligned priorities, and delayed communications can quickly compound into major project risks. On the other hand, a well-integrated team—supported by the right tools—can respond faster, make better decisions, and maintain high productivity.

The Role of Tools in Enabling Seamless Collaboration

Collaboration isn't just about people—it's also about the platforms that enable them to work better together. Jira and Confluence, when used independently, already provide robust functionality for task management and documentation. But when integrated, they become a powerhouse that bridges the gap between planning and execution.

- **Jira** ensures that tasks, sprints, and development work are organized and trackable.
- **Confluence** captures knowledge, discussions, and decision-making context in a transparent, shareable format.
- Together, they allow teams to plan, act, and learn—*all in one place*.

By seamlessly integrating these tools, teams eliminate redundant workflows, improve visibility, and accelerate delivery cycles—all without compromising quality or accountability.

The Human Factor: Fostering a Collaborative Culture

While tools are vital, seamless collaboration also requires a mindset shift. Leaders must champion openness, shared responsibility, and continuous improvement. Teams must be encouraged to communicate early and often, document everything, and align around shared goals. When culture and tools align, collaboration becomes second nature rather than a forced process.

Laying the Foundation for This Book

This chapter sets the tone for the rest of the book. In the chapters that follow, you'll learn how to understand, prepare, implement, and optimize the integration of Jira and Confluence. The goal is not just technical proficiency—but to empower you to lead and nurture a truly collaborative project environment.

With the right strategies and execution, seamless collaboration isn't just possible—it's *inevitable*. And it starts here.

Why Jira and Confluence Together?

A Powerful Duo for Modern Project Management

In the realm of project management, efficiency, transparency, and adaptability are crucial. Individually, **Jira** and **Confluence** offer powerful features that help teams plan, execute, and document their work. But when used together, these tools create a synergistic environment that not only enhances productivity but also fosters seamless collaboration across departments and workflows.

Jira and Confluence are both developed by Atlassian and are designed to complement one another. While Jira specializes in **issue tracking, task management, and agile project execution**, Confluence is geared towards **documentation, knowledge sharing, and real-time team collaboration**. Integrating the two provides a complete project ecosystem—from idea to delivery.

Bridging Execution and Documentation

A common pain point in many organizations is the disconnection between planning and execution. Engineers may be working in Jira, while project managers and stakeholders rely on documents, meeting notes, and static reports in separate platforms. This fragmentation leads to delays, miscommunication, and a lack of alignment.

When Jira and Confluence are integrated:

- **Jira issues and progress can be referenced or embedded directly in Confluence pages**, eliminating duplication of information.
- **Project documentation can be dynamically updated**, ensuring everyone is working with the latest insights.
- **Sprint retrospectives, release notes, and project reports** can be auto-generated from real-time Jira data, saving hours of manual effort.

This bridge between execution and documentation is what transforms isolated productivity into collaborative success.

Centralized Knowledge and Agile Execution

Confluence acts as the **single source of truth** for team knowledge—hosting everything from product requirement documents (PRDs) and meeting summaries to how-to guides and retrospectives. Jira, on the other hand, ensures **tasks are actionable, measurable, and traceable**.

When combined:

- Product managers can link requirements in Confluence directly to development tasks in Jira.
- QA teams can trace test cases written in Confluence to issues in Jira.
- Stakeholders gain visibility into both **what is being built** (in Jira) and **why it's being built** (in Confluence).

This integration not only improves **traceability** and **accountability** but also enhances **cross-team collaboration** by giving every stakeholder access to relevant, contextual information.

Increased Transparency and Efficiency

By working in tandem, Jira and Confluence eliminate information silos. Team members don't have to ask where something is documented or track down the latest updates. Everyone—from developers and designers to marketers and executives—can stay informed through **centralized dashboards, live reports, and linked content**.

This improved transparency leads to:

- **Faster decision-making**
- **Reduced misunderstandings**
- **Increased team alignment**
- **Shorter feedback loops**

Moreover, automations between Jira and Confluence help reduce repetitive tasks and allow teams to focus on strategic execution instead of manual updates.

Preparing for Scalable Collaboration

As teams grow and projects scale, maintaining alignment becomes increasingly difficult. Having Jira and Confluence work together sets the foundation for **scalable, sustainable collaboration**. Whether your team is co-located or remote, small or enterprise-scale, this integration ensures everyone is operating from a shared, up-to-date context.

Whether you're managing agile software development, marketing campaigns, or cross-functional initiatives, Jira and Confluence offer unmatched capabilities when integrated thoughtfully.

Setting the Stage for This Book

This chapter highlights why Jira and Confluence are better together—but it's only the beginning. The rest of this book will take you through everything you need to know to **integrate**, **customize**, and **optimize** your project management framework using these two tools. By the end, you'll not only understand how to make them work together—you'll know how to make them *work for you*.

Target Audience and How to Use This Book

Who This Book Is For

This book is designed for professionals who are serious about enhancing team collaboration and project efficiency through the power of integrated tools. Whether you're a seasoned project manager or a tech-savvy team leader, if you're looking to streamline communication, documentation, and task execution, this guide is for you.

Specifically, this book caters to:

- **Project Managers and Scrum Masters** Seeking to align planning, execution, and documentation in a single ecosystem.
- **Agile Teams and Product Owners** Aiming to maintain a transparent backlog, track progress, and document decisions in real time.
- **Software Developers and QA Engineers** Looking to collaborate better by linking tasks to documentation, specs, and test cases.
- **Business Analysts and Documentation Specialists** Who want to build a knowledge hub that stays in sync with project updates.
- **Team Leads and Department Heads** Working to scale their team's operations while maintaining structure, clarity, and accountability.
- **IT Admins and System Integrators** Responsible for configuring, maintaining, and securing integrated toolchains.

You don't need to be an expert in Jira or Confluence to benefit from this book. If you've used either tool before—or even if you're just getting started—this guide will help you move from basic understanding to confident implementation.

What This Book Covers

This book follows a clear, progressive structure to walk you through **understanding**, **preparing for**, **implementing**, and **optimizing** the integration between Jira and Confluence.

Here's how the chapters are structured:

- **Introduction**: Outlines the significance of seamless collaboration and the unique value of integrating Jira with Confluence.
- **Foundations**: Gives you a working understanding of both tools and their roles in project management.
- **Preparation**: Helps you assess your current workflow, identify integration goals, and prepare stakeholders.
- **Integration Strategies**: Breaks down the core ways in which the two platforms can be connected and customized.
- **Implementation**: Offers step-by-step guidance on setup, templates, macros, and migrating data.
- **Collaboration Workflows**: Shows how to apply integration in everyday activities like sprint planning and documentation.
- **Advanced Techniques**: Explores automations, APIs, scripts, and apps for power users who want to take things further.
- **Troubleshooting & Optimization**: Addresses common issues and performance tips for larger teams.
- **Real-World Use Cases**: Provides examples of how different types of teams benefit from integration.
- **Scaling & Future-Proofing**: Prepares you for growth, updates, and emerging technologies like AI.

How to Use This Book

You can read this book from start to finish if you're new to Jira-Confluence integration and want a comprehensive understanding. However, it's also designed for **modular use**—feel free to jump to the sections most relevant to your current needs.

- **New to Both Tools?** Start with Sections 1 and 2.
- **Already Using Jira or Confluence Separately?** Focus on Sections 3 and 4 to begin integrating.
- **Looking to Optimize Existing Setups?** Head to Sections 6 and 7.
- **Need Inspiration from Real Teams?** See the use cases in Section 8.

Each chapter is written to be **concise, practical, and actionable**—fitting comfortably within a few A4-sized pages to avoid information overload. The goal is to help you implement strategies quickly and confidently.

Final Thought

Whether you're leading a small team or scaling operations across an enterprise, the insights in this book will help you unlock the full potential of Jira and Confluence as a **unified collaboration system**.

Let's get started.

Section 1:
Understanding Jira and Confluence Fundamentals

Jira 101: Core Features for Project Management

Introduction to Jira

Jira, developed by Atlassian, is one of the most widely used project management tools, particularly favored by agile software development teams. However, its flexibility makes it suitable for a wide range of industries and workflows. At its core, Jira helps teams **track tasks, manage workflows, and ensure accountability** throughout a project's lifecycle.

In this chapter, we'll walk through the **fundamental features of Jira** that form the backbone of efficient, transparent project management. Whether you're leading a team, managing tasks, or simply trying to bring order to chaos, understanding Jira's core capabilities is essential before integrating it with Confluence.

Issue Types: The Building Blocks

In Jira, every task or piece of work is represented as an **issue**. These aren't necessarily "problems" but rather **units of work**. Common issue types include:

- **Story**: A feature or requirement from a user's perspective.
- **Task**: A general work item.
- **Bug**: A defect that needs fixing.
- **Epic**: A large body of work that can be broken down into smaller issues.
- **Sub-task**: A granular piece of work that belongs to a parent issue.

This issue hierarchy helps teams break down large goals into manageable actions, while maintaining traceability.

Boards: Visual Workflow Management

Jira provides **Scrum boards** and **Kanban boards** to visualize work in progress. These boards are tied to workflows and allow teams to:

- View tasks across different stages (e.g., To Do, In Progress, Done)
- Prioritize issues in the backlog
- Manage sprint planning and execution
- Identify bottlenecks in the workflow

Boards are interactive and provide real-time visibility into what's happening across the team, which supports better planning and coordination.

Workflows: Defining Process

Jira's power lies in its ability to **customize workflows**—the set of statuses and transitions that an issue goes through from creation to completion. Workflows help enforce team processes by:

- Standardizing how issues move through different stages
- Triggering events, such as notifications or field updates
- Automating repetitive steps with conditions and validators

By modeling real-world processes, workflows ensure consistency, accountability, and clarity in project execution.

Agile Tools and Sprints

For teams practicing Agile, Jira offers robust support:

- **Backlogs**: Prioritized lists of user stories and tasks
- **Sprints**: Time-boxed periods where teams commit to specific work
- **Burndown Charts**: Visualizations of progress toward sprint goals
- **Velocity Reports**: Insights into team output over time

These tools help teams iterate effectively, measure progress, and continuously improve their delivery cycle.

Permissions and Roles

Jira offers granular **permission schemes** to control who can view, create, edit, and transition issues. Roles like **Project Administrator, Developer, Tester**, and **Viewer** can be assigned to ensure security and accountability.

This flexibility is especially important for organizations that need to manage access across multiple departments or client-facing environments.

Filters and Dashboards

Jira allows users to create **custom filters** using JQL (Jira Query Language) to find issues based on specific criteria. These filters can be saved and shared, forming the basis for powerful:

- **Dashboards**: Personalized views showing charts, statistics, and activity
- **Reports**: Sprint reviews, issue distributions, and team workload analysis
- **Automation Rules**: Triggered actions based on filtered results

With filters and dashboards, teams get **real-time insights** into project health and individual performance.

Integration Readiness

Understanding these core features is not only essential for using Jira effectively but also for **preparing it for integration with Confluence**. When both platforms are aligned, you can:

- Reference issues directly in documentation
- Display dynamic Jira reports on Confluence pages
- Automate status updates and progress tracking across tools

Mastering the fundamentals of Jira ensures you're ready to leverage its full potential—especially when integrated into a collaborative ecosystem with Confluence.

Summary

Jira is more than a task tracker—it's a **strategic platform for planning, executing, and improving team workflows**. From issue tracking and agile boards to custom workflows and reporting tools, Jira equips teams to work smarter, faster, and with greater transparency.

Confluence 101: Building a Knowledge Hub

Introduction to Confluence

While Jira excels at tracking tasks and managing agile workflows, **Confluence** serves as the collaborative space where ideas are formed, documented, and shared. Developed by Atlassian, Confluence is a **knowledge management and team collaboration tool** designed to centralize your organization's content in one accessible place.

In this chapter, we'll explore the core features of Confluence and how it enables teams to build a **structured, searchable, and collaborative knowledge hub**—a vital counterpart to the execution-focused Jira platform.

The Purpose of a Knowledge Hub

In modern project management, documentation is just as important as task execution. Teams need a place to:

- Record project requirements and decisions
- Share meeting notes, action items, and follow-ups
- Maintain process documentation and best practices
- Store training materials and onboarding guides
- Collaborate on content in real time

A **knowledge hub** is more than just a content repository—it's a **living, evolving space** that keeps everyone aligned, informed, and empowered to contribute.

Pages and Spaces: Organizing Content

At the heart of Confluence are **pages** and **spaces**:

- **Pages** are where you create and edit content—project plans, documentation, FAQs, etc.
- **Spaces** are collections of pages, typically organized by team, department, or project.

This hierarchy ensures a clean, navigable structure. For example, a software team might have a space for "Development" with pages for sprint retrospectives, release plans, and API documentation.

Pages support **rich content formatting**, including text, images, tables, file attachments, and dynamic elements like task lists and roadmaps—making them ideal for both static documentation and collaborative planning.

Templates and Blueprints

To streamline content creation, Confluence offers **templates and blueprints** that help standardize recurring documents. These include:

- Meeting Notes
- Product Requirements
- Decision Logs
- Project Plans
- Retrospectives

You can also create **custom templates** tailored to your organization's workflows. This ensures consistency across teams and encourages documentation as a habitual part of your project process.

Real-Time Collaboration

Confluence promotes a **collaborative writing environment** where multiple team members can edit pages simultaneously. With features like:

- Inline commenting
- Page history and version control
- Mentions using @username
- Collaborative checklists and task assignments

It becomes easier to capture input from diverse stakeholders and iterate on content without losing traceability.

This collaborative nature reduces the reliance on emails, scattered documents, or outdated spreadsheets—keeping everything **centralized and accessible**.

Search and Discoverability

One of Confluence's most valuable features is its **powerful search engine**. Every page, comment, and attachment is indexed, allowing users to quickly find the information they need. Tags, labels, and page hierarchies further enhance discoverability, ensuring that no knowledge is lost or buried.

This is especially crucial as teams scale and accumulate more content over time.

Integration with Jira

Confluence is designed to work seamlessly with Jira. Once integrated, you can:

- **Embed Jira issues or boards directly into pages**
- **Generate automatic reports based on Jira data**
- **Link documentation to specific Jira epics or stories**
- **Track development progress from within Confluence**

This connection transforms Confluence from a static documentation tool into a **dynamic project companion**, reflecting real-time changes from Jira and providing complete context for every task.

Customization and Access Control

Confluence allows space admins to define **permission levels** to control who can view, edit, or comment on content. This enables sensitive information to be restricted while allowing open collaboration where appropriate.

Pages can also be **organized using page trees**, nested hierarchies, and navigation menus to suit your team's structure and preferences.

Summary

Confluence is the **digital workspace** where knowledge is created, curated, and continuously improved. It complements Jira by handling everything that lives *around* the task: the plans, the discussions, the learnings, and the documentation.

When used effectively, Confluence becomes the **single source of truth** for your team—reducing friction, boosting productivity, and laying the groundwork for seamless collaboration across your entire organization.

The Role of Jira in Agile Workflows

Why Agile Needs Structure

Agile project management thrives on adaptability, collaboration, and continuous delivery. But without a structured system to organize work, track progress, and maintain visibility, even the most agile teams can quickly lose direction. That's where **Jira** becomes an indispensable tool. Jira provides the structure that Agile needs—without compromising flexibility.

This chapter explores how Jira empowers Agile teams to **plan, track, and iterate** effectively while maintaining full transparency throughout the development cycle.

Backlogs: Managing the Flow of Work

Every Agile journey begins with a well-organized **backlog**. In Jira, the product backlog serves as a central repository for user stories, tasks, bugs, and epics. It helps teams:

- Prioritize upcoming work
- Define sprint goals
- Break down large initiatives into manageable chunks

Each backlog item is represented as a **Jira issue**, complete with detailed descriptions, labels, priorities, and estimates—making it easy to organize, assign, and refine tasks collaboratively.

Sprint Planning and Execution

Jira streamlines sprint planning by allowing teams to:

- Select a subset of backlog items for an upcoming sprint
- Assign story points or time estimates
- Allocate tasks to specific team members
- Define sprint goals and set the sprint duration

Once a sprint begins, Jira tracks all related activities, helping the team monitor progress through **Scrum boards** that reflect the workflow (e.g., To Do → In Progress → Done).

Jira's **active sprint view** provides real-time visibility into work status, blockers, and team capacity—enabling quick course corrections when needed.

Kanban for Continuous Delivery

In addition to Scrum, Jira supports **Kanban**, a lean project management method ideal for continuous delivery teams. Jira Kanban boards allow:

- Continuous prioritization and delivery
- Work-in-progress (WIP) limits to prevent bottlenecks
- Immediate visibility into each task's current stage

Kanban teams benefit from Jira's ability to visualize flow and reduce cycle times while maintaining productivity across fast-moving projects.

Agile Reporting and Metrics

One of Jira's biggest advantages for Agile teams is its built-in reporting capabilities. These include:

- **Burndown Charts**: Visualize remaining work and sprint progress

- **Velocity Charts**: Analyze team performance over past sprints
- **Cumulative Flow Diagrams**: Track work item status trends
- **Sprint Reports**: Review what was completed and what carried over

These reports help teams **reflect, improve, and plan better**, making retrospectives more data-driven and actionable.

Custom Workflows for Agile Flexibility

Agile isn't one-size-fits-all—and Jira respects that. Teams can define **custom workflows** tailored to their development style. Whether you're following Scrum, Kanban, Scrumban, or a hybrid approach, Jira allows you to:

- Add or rename workflow statuses
- Create custom transitions with conditions and validations
- Automate status updates and notifications

This adaptability ensures Jira fits *your* process—not the other way around.

Collaboration and Transparency

Jira enhances team communication through:

- @Mentions and comments for contextual discussions
- Real-time notifications and activity feeds
- Integration with Slack, MS Teams, and Confluence for centralized updates

These features promote transparency and reduce the need for redundant status meetings, allowing teams to focus more on delivery.

Linking Work to Strategic Goals

Agile isn't just about development speed—it's also about alignment. Jira supports **epic and initiative-level tracking**, enabling teams to:

- Tie individual tasks to larger business objectives
- Ensure development work aligns with strategic goals
- Maintain traceability from idea to release

For scaled Agile frameworks like SAFe or LeSS, Jira integrates with advanced planning tools (like Advanced Roadmaps) to provide a top-down view of the portfolio.

Summary

Jira isn't just a task tracker—it's a **dynamic Agile engine**. From managing backlogs and running sprints to tracking metrics and enabling collaboration, Jira gives Agile teams the tools they need to **move fast, stay focused, and deliver value continuously**.

The Role of Confluence in Documentation and Planning

The Foundation of Clarity and Alignment

Every successful project is built not just on efficient task execution but also on **clear communication, comprehensive documentation, and deliberate planning**. While Jira is the go-to tool for tracking work and managing sprints, **Confluence plays a complementary role by supporting the creation, organization, and sharing of knowledge and plans** across teams.

In this chapter, we'll explore how Confluence serves as a critical hub for documentation and planning, enabling teams to stay aligned, transparent, and productive throughout the project lifecycle.

Turning Ideas into Actionable Plans

Project planning begins long before tasks are created in Jira. It starts with brainstorming, defining objectives, understanding requirements, and establishing scope. Confluence offers a collaborative canvas to:

- Draft and iterate on **project charters** and **planning documents**
- Document **meeting notes, agendas**, and **follow-ups**
- Align on **goals, timelines, and stakeholder expectations**
- Capture **decisions** and **rationales** in one accessible location

Using structured **page templates**—such as product requirement docs (PRDs), roadmaps, or project briefs—teams can quickly spin up reusable formats that promote consistency and clarity.

Collaborative Documentation in Real Time

Unlike traditional document tools, Confluence is built for **real-time, multi-user collaboration**. Team members can:

- Co-edit pages simultaneously
- Leave inline comments and suggestions
- Tag team members with @mentions for input or review
- Track changes through **version history** and **page comparison**

This live, iterative editing environment ensures that everyone stays on the same page—literally and figuratively—while reducing back-and-forth emails and versioning chaos.

Creating a Living Knowledge Base

Documentation in Confluence isn't static—it evolves with your project. As plans change or insights emerge, teams can continuously update:

- Process guides
- Onboarding materials
- Feature specifications
- Lessons learned
- Support FAQs

Organized into **spaces** and **nested page trees**, Confluence makes it easy to maintain a living knowledge base that supports both ongoing work and future reference.

This becomes especially powerful for remote teams or growing organizations, where quick access to accurate information can make the difference between momentum and misalignment.

Planning Sprints and Releases

Confluence isn't just for high-level planning—it also supports detailed execution plans. Teams often use Confluence to:

- Define **sprint goals** and **release checklists**
- Plan **sprint retrospectives** and **post-mortems**
- Outline **testing strategies** and **rollout plans**
- Document **acceptance criteria** and **technical constraints**

When paired with Jira, you can **link relevant Jira issues directly within Confluence pages**, allowing for traceability between what was planned and what is being done.

Enhancing Transparency and Alignment

One of the biggest benefits of using Confluence for documentation and planning is its ability to **break down silos**. By centralizing information:

- Stakeholders can monitor project status without interrupting the team
- New hires or cross-functional collaborators can get up to speed faster
- Decisions and context remain preserved for future reference

With **powerful search**, **tags**, and **navigation structures**, teams can find what they need—when they need it—without wading through emails or outdated folders.

Linking Strategy to Execution

Confluence acts as the **bridge between high-level strategy and Jira task execution**. Planning pages provide context and rationale, while Jira handles granular work items. By integrating both tools:

- Confluence pages can show real-time **Jira reports** (like sprint progress or issue status)
- Jira issues can link back to relevant **documentation or meeting notes**
- Project dashboards can combine **status, goals, blockers, and decisions** in one place

This unified visibility ensures that execution remains aligned with planning throughout the project lifecycle.

Summary

Confluence plays a critical role in **capturing knowledge, documenting plans, and aligning teams**. While Jira powers the "how" of project execution, Confluence empowers the "why" and "what"—providing structure, transparency, and collaboration in the planning and documentation process.

In the next section, we'll explore how to **prepare for integration** by assessing your team's collaboration needs, aligning stakeholders, and laying the groundwork for a smooth Jira-Confluence setup.

Section 2:
Preparing for Integration

Assessing Your Team's Collaboration Needs

Setting the Stage for Integration Success

Before diving into integration, automation, or workflow enhancements, it's essential to take a step back and assess what your team *actually needs*. Integrating Jira with Confluence can offer transformative benefits—but only when it's tailored to your team's specific challenges, processes, and goals.

This chapter helps you analyze your current collaboration environment so you can **approach integration intentionally**, ensuring it solves real problems rather than adding complexity.

Why Assessment Matters

Many teams jump into integration based on features or technical capabilities, only to realize later that their setup doesn't align with how they work. A thoughtful needs assessment helps you:

- Avoid tool fatigue or misuse
- Focus on outcomes over features
- Maximize user adoption and ROI
- Streamline workflows rather than complicate them

This process also helps build internal alignment—getting buy-in from stakeholders, team leads, and end users before changes are introduced.

Step 1: Understand Your Current Tool Landscape

Start by listing the tools currently used for:

- Task tracking (e.g., Jira, Trello, Excel)
- Documentation (e.g., Confluence, Google Docs, Notion)
- Communication (e.g., Slack, Teams, Email)
- Reporting and dashboards (e.g., Excel, Power BI, third-party apps)

Evaluate how these tools work together—or don't. Ask:

- Are your teams duplicating effort across platforms?
- Is information scattered or hard to find?
- Do tools support or hinder transparency and visibility?
- Are stakeholders accessing real-time updates or outdated summaries?

Understanding your current ecosystem sets the baseline for improvement.

Step 2: Identify Collaboration Pain Points

Talk to team members across roles and levels. Some useful questions include:

- Where do communication gaps most often occur?
- Are tasks frequently delayed due to lack of context or documentation?
- How are sprint or release plans tracked and shared?
- How much time is spent looking for information?
- Do teams struggle with version control or outdated files?

Capture feedback in a structured format—like a table or categorized list—to spot recurring issues that integration could address.

Step 3: Analyze Team Structure and Workflow

Different teams collaborate in different ways. Map out how your team typically:

- Plans a project
- Documents requirements
- Assigns and tracks tasks
- Reviews progress and reports outcomes
- Handles retrospectives and continuous improvement

Identify if these processes vary across departments (e.g., engineering vs. marketing) and whether a unified collaboration strategy is feasible—or whether flexible setups are needed for different groups.

Also, consider how distributed or remote your team is. Hybrid and remote teams often benefit the most from centralized tools like Jira and Confluence.

Step 4: Define Integration Goals

Once you've diagnosed the collaboration gaps and inefficiencies, define specific goals for integrating Jira and Confluence. For example:

- "Create a single source of truth for sprint planning and documentation."
- "Reduce time spent updating stakeholders by linking Jira issues to Confluence reports."
- "Improve visibility into sprint status for non-technical stakeholders."
- "Eliminate duplication of meeting notes and development progress."

Having clear, measurable goals helps guide your configuration choices and ensures you're building for outcomes—not just functionality.

Step 5: Determine Stakeholder Requirements

Different roles have different needs. Make sure to include:

- **Project Managers** who need real-time visibility and reporting
- **Developers** who want minimal context-switching and clear task linkage
- **QA/Testers** who require traceability between test plans and tasks
- **Executives/Stakeholders** who want high-level dashboards without technical detail
- **New team members** who need easy onboarding and documentation access

Gathering these diverse requirements ensures that your integration supports all contributors—not just the technical team.

Step 6: Evaluate Readiness for Change

Lastly, assess your team's openness to adopting an integrated workflow. Consider:

- Is there a culture of documentation and knowledge sharing?
- Are teams currently disciplined in Jira usage?
- Is leadership supportive of tooling improvements?
- Do you have champions or power users to lead adoption?

If gaps exist, you may need to introduce change gradually or provide training alongside rollout to ensure success.

Summary

Integration isn't just about connecting tools—it's about **aligning technology with people and process**. By thoroughly assessing your team's collaboration needs, you ensure that the Jira-Confluence integration is not only technically sound, but *strategically effective*.

Prerequisites for Integrating Jira and Confluence

Laying the Groundwork for a Smooth Integration

Before you can fully leverage the synergy between Jira and Confluence, there are a number of **technical, administrative, and organizational prerequisites** that must be in place. Skipping this preparation can lead to misconfigurations, access issues, and low adoption rates.

This chapter outlines what you need to have ready—both technically and strategically—so your integration is seamless, secure, and aligned with your team's goals.

1. Compatible Hosting Environment

Jira and Confluence are available in multiple deployment models:

- **Cloud** (hosted by Atlassian)
- **Data Center** (self-managed, for large enterprises)
- **Server** (legacy; support ending soon)

For the most seamless integration with minimal setup, **Jira Cloud and Confluence Cloud** are recommended. Atlassian's cloud products offer out-of-the-box integration, frequent updates, and lower maintenance overhead.

Tip: Ensure both tools are on compatible hosting environments. Integrating Cloud with Server requires third-party apps or complex configurations.

2. Admin Access to Both Platforms

To configure integration features like linking issues, embedding reports, and syncing permissions, you need:

- **Site Admin access** to Jira and Confluence
- Ability to manage global permissions and add-ons
- Access to product settings for API tokens and webhooks (if needed)

Without the right admin permissions, you'll be limited in how deeply the platforms can be integrated.

3. Verified User Management Setup

Jira and Confluence users must be **consistently managed**, especially if you plan to use unified permissions or single sign-on (SSO). Recommended practices include:

- Centralized user management via **Atlassian Admin (Cloud)**
- Groups or roles that map across both tools
- Email domains verified and access restrictions applied where needed

Proper user provisioning ensures that collaboration features like @mentions, issue linking, and commenting work smoothly.

4. Defined Project and Space Structures

Integration is most effective when Jira projects and Confluence spaces are **aligned**. Before setting up links, ensure:

- Each Jira project has a corresponding Confluence space (or section)
- Naming conventions are consistent and logical
- Team members understand where to find relevant documentation

This alignment simplifies issue linking, cross-referencing, and dashboard creation.

---

5. Content Organization Strategy

To avoid disorganized or overlapping content after integration, define a **clear content structure** in advance:

- What content belongs in Confluence (e.g., specs, meeting notes)?
- What content belongs in Jira (e.g., tasks, bugs, epics)?
- How will they link together (e.g., page links, embedded filters)?
- Who owns documentation, and how often is it updated?

Having these standards helps ensure the system is scalable and intuitive for everyone.

---

6. Training and Onboarding Plan

A successful integration isn't just technical—it's also cultural. Prepare a **brief onboarding plan** for your team that covers:

- How to link Jira issues to Confluence pages
- How to embed Jira reports into Confluence
- When to document in Confluence vs. log tasks in Jira
- Best practices for naming, tagging, and updating content

This ensures everyone understands the tools, reducing confusion and increasing adoption.

---

7. Optional but Recommended: Marketplace Add-ons

While the native integration covers most basic needs, you may also want to explore Atlassian Marketplace apps that enhance the experience, such as:

- **Advanced Tables for Confluence**
- **Jira Snapshots for Confluence**
- **Automation for Jira**
- **Macros for richer reporting and visualization**

These tools can fill specific gaps or add more flexibility to your integration.

---

8. Internal Stakeholder Alignment

Finally, ensure all key stakeholders—such as team leads, project managers, IT admins, and department heads—are aligned on:

- Why the integration is happening
- What problems it's solving
- How success will be measured
- What the rollout and support process will look like

This alignment avoids resistance, helps allocate the right resources, and makes post-integration improvements easier to manage.

Summary

Successful integration begins with proper preparation. From confirming hosting compatibility and admin access to aligning projects, organizing content, and preparing your team, these prerequisites lay the **foundation for a powerful, unified collaboration system**.

Aligning Stakeholders and Setting Expectations

Collaboration Begins with Clarity

Even the most technically sound integration between Jira and Confluence can fall short if people aren't aligned. Successful implementation depends not just on tools—but on **people, communication, and shared understanding**.

This chapter focuses on the importance of aligning all stakeholders and setting clear expectations before you move into actual configuration. It's about **building consensus, minimizing resistance, and ensuring sustained adoption**.

Why Stakeholder Alignment Matters

Integration affects more than just developers or admins—it touches **product managers, team leads, executives, business analysts, testers**, and even clients. Misalignment at this stage can result in:

- Conflicting expectations
- Fragmented usage across teams
- Resistance to change
- Poor adoption and ROI

Clear alignment ensures that integration efforts deliver meaningful value for all involved.

Step 1: Identify Your Stakeholders

Begin by mapping out everyone who will interact with Jira and Confluence, or who has a vested interest in how projects are managed. This may include:

- **Project Managers** (concerned with planning and reporting)
- **Product Owners** (managing requirements and user stories)
- **Developers and QA Teams** (executing work and tracking issues)
- **Business Analysts** (documenting workflows and specs)
- **Department Heads or Executives** (seeking visibility and KPIs)
- **IT and Security Teams** (handling access and compliance)
- **End Users or Clients** (consuming reports or participating in reviews)

This inclusive approach prevents blind spots and builds a foundation of trust across roles.

Step 2: Communicate the Value Proposition

Once stakeholders are identified, tailor your communication to their interests. Explain how the integration will:

- **Improve transparency** across teams and departments
- **Eliminate redundant work** and disconnected tools
- **Enhance productivity** with real-time updates and traceability
- **Support better decision-making** through unified reporting
- **Enable long-term scalability** for growing teams and projects

Focus on **outcomes** instead of technical details. People support what they understand and believe in.

Step 3: Define Roles and Responsibilities

A successful integration initiative must have clear ownership. Clarify:

- **Who will lead the integration project?**
- **Who will configure and test the systems?**
- **Who will provide training and support?**
- **Who will maintain and update documentation?**
- **Who will gather feedback post-rollout?**

Assigning roles reduces ambiguity, accelerates decision-making, and ensures accountability during setup and beyond.

Step 4: Set Realistic Expectations

Stakeholders often have different assumptions about what the integration will achieve. Address this by defining:

- **What the integration will include at launch** (e.g., issue linking, dashboards, real-time reports)
- **What features or phases will come later** (e.g., automation rules, API customization)
- **What limitations exist** (e.g., platform constraints, user training needs)
- **What success looks like**, including clear KPIs or adoption goals

Example expectations might include:

- "All sprint planning documents will be maintained in Confluence and linked to Jira issues."
- "Product requirement pages must include embedded Jira filters for traceability."
- "Dashboards for leadership will be auto-generated weekly using Confluence macros."

These agreements reduce surprises and help manage both timelines and perceptions.

Step 5: Establish Feedback Loops

Integration is not a one-time setup—it's an evolving system. Set up processes to:

- **Collect feedback regularly** through surveys, meetings, or Confluence forms
- **Review performance metrics** (e.g., usage stats, page views, ticket resolution times)
- **Adapt the system** based on what's working and what isn't

This builds a culture of continuous improvement and gives stakeholders a voice in shaping the tools they use daily.

Step 6: Get Early Buy-In with a Pilot Group

Before rolling out integration across the entire organization, consider launching with a **pilot team**. Choose a group that is:

- Representative of broader use cases

- Open to change and experimentation
- Able to provide actionable feedback

This phased approach allows you to fine-tune your setup, demonstrate quick wins, and gather testimonials that can help drive adoption organization-wide.

Summary

Aligning stakeholders and setting expectations isn't a formality—it's a **strategic step that determines the success of your integration**. By engaging the right people, clarifying goals, assigning responsibilities, and managing expectations, you lay the groundwork for a rollout that's both smooth and impactful.

Choosing the Right Integration Approach

Tailoring Integration to Your Team's Needs

Integrating Jira with Confluence isn't a one-size-fits-all process. Different teams have different collaboration styles, security needs, technical expertise, and scalability goals. Choosing the **right integration approach** is critical to ensuring your tools support your workflow rather than complicate it.

In this chapter, we'll explore the **core integration methods** available, weigh their pros and cons, and guide you through selecting the approach that best suits your environment and business objectives.

What Does "Integration" Really Mean?

At its core, integrating Jira and Confluence means **creating a seamless, bidirectional link** between work execution and documentation. The level of integration can vary, including:

- Linking individual Jira issues to specific Confluence pages
- Embedding dynamic Jira boards or reports inside Confluence
- Automating updates and syncing permissions across platforms
- Creating custom workflows or dashboards that draw data from both tools

Your approach will depend on **how deeply you want the systems to talk to each other**, and what business value you're trying to unlock.

Integration Methods Overview

1. Native Atlassian Cloud Integration (Recommended for Most Teams)

Atlassian provides **built-in, plug-and-play integration features** for Jira Cloud and Confluence Cloud users.

Features:

- Embed Jira issues, lists, and charts into Confluence pages
- Link Confluence pages to Jira epics or stories
- View Confluence content within Jira issue panels
- Use Jira macros in Confluence for live data reports

Best For:

- Teams using **both products in the Cloud**
- Organizations seeking **quick setup** and **low maintenance**
- Non-technical teams that want functionality without scripting

Pros:

- No add-ons required
- Seamless user experience
- Secure and regularly updated by Atlassian
- Quick to deploy

Cons:

- Limited customization beyond the default macros
- May not support hybrid Cloud-Server setups

---

2. Marketplace Add-ons and Connectors

Atlassian Marketplace offers **enhanced integration plugins** like *Jira Snapshots for Confluence, Advanced Tables,* or *Projectrak for Jira.*

Features:

- Advanced reporting options
- Snapshot-based data tracking
- Greater layout and data visualization control
- Extended automation between platforms

Best For:

- Teams with **specific use cases** (e.g., compliance tracking, cross-project reporting)
- Organizations needing **flexibility** beyond native tools

Pros:

- Tailored functionality
- Often extend Jira-Confluence interaction without scripting
- Regularly supported by third-party developers

Cons:

- Adds cost and dependency on third parties
- May require additional user training
- Compatibility varies across Cloud and Data Center versions

---

3. Custom API Integration

For advanced teams, Atlassian's REST APIs allow **fully customized, programmatic integrations**.

Use Cases:

- Automating workflows between Jira and Confluence
- Pushing/pulling data between tools and external platforms (e.g., CRMs, data warehouses)
- Building internal dashboards or reporting systems

Best For:

- Technical teams with **developer resources**
- Organizations needing **integration with non-Atlassian tools**
- Enterprises building **custom automation or BI solutions**

Pros:

- Maximum control
- Infinite customization potential
- Can connect with other tools in your tech stack

Cons:

- Requires coding expertise
- Higher initial effort and ongoing maintenance
- Risk of breaking changes with API updates

---

4. Manual Linking and Basic Usage

For small teams or organizations just starting out, **manual linking** between Jira issues and Confluence pages is a valid first step.

How it works:

- Users manually copy Jira issue links into Confluence pages
- Use simple text references or URLs
- No macros or embedded data

Best For:

- Small teams or short-term projects
- Teams evaluating integration benefits before committing to full setup

Pros:

- No technical setup required
- Easy to implement immediately

Cons:

- No real-time data updates
- Risk of outdated or inconsistent information
- Not scalable for long-term or larger teams

How to Choose the Best Approach

Ask yourself these questions:

1. **Where are your Jira and Confluence hosted?**
   - If both are on **Cloud**, start with native integration.
   - If you use **Server or Data Center**, verify plugin compatibility.
2. **What is your team's technical capability?**
   - Non-technical teams should stick to built-in features or visual add-ons.
   - Technical teams may explore APIs for automation and cross-platform workflows.
3. **How complex are your reporting or workflow needs?**
   - For basic dashboards and status tracking, native macros will suffice.
   - For advanced metrics, cross-project views, or external syncing, consider add-ons or APIs.
4. **What is your budget and timeline?**
   - Built-in features are free and quick to set up.
   - Add-ons and APIs require time and financial investment.
5. **Do you need scalability and compliance?**
   - Larger teams and enterprise environments often benefit from add-ons or APIs that allow detailed permissions, automation, and reporting.

Hybrid and Phased Approaches

You don't have to start with a full integration from day one. Many successful teams adopt a **phased strategy**:

1. Begin with **native integration** (linking issues, embedding reports)
2. Gradually introduce **templates and dashboards**
3. Layer in **marketplace apps or automation tools**
4. Scale up to **custom integrations** as needed

This strategy ensures your team gets familiar with core features while laying the groundwork for future growth.

Summary

Choosing the right integration approach means balancing **capability, simplicity, scalability, and effort**. Whether you're using built-in tools, third-party add-ons, or building your own workflows, the key is to **align the solution with your team's current and future needs**.

In the next section, we'll dive into **Core Integration Strategies**—starting with how to link Jira issues to Confluence pages for real-time context and collaboration.

Section 3:
Core Integration Strategies

Linking Jira Issues to Confluence Pages

Bridging Execution and Documentation

At the heart of effective project collaboration is **contextual visibility**—the ability to see not just *what* is being worked on, but *why* it matters and *how* it fits into the broader plan. Linking Jira issues to Confluence pages creates a dynamic connection between **task execution** and **project documentation**, giving teams a unified workspace where decisions, updates, and progress coexist.

In this chapter, we'll explore the strategic benefits, practical use cases, and step-by-step instructions for linking Jira issues to Confluence pages. Whether you're managing user stories, documenting product requirements, or tracking sprint retrospectives, this foundational integration enhances transparency and efficiency across your workflows.

Why Linking Matters

Linking Jira issues to Confluence pages enables:

- **Real-time status tracking within documentation**
- **Seamless navigation between tasks and related context**
- **Reduced duplication of information**
- **Improved stakeholder visibility**
- **Faster onboarding and fewer communication gaps**

When used consistently, this strategy ensures that **plans remain actionable** and **tasks stay informed by purpose**.

Common Use Cases

Here are some practical ways teams use Jira-Confluence linking:

- **Product Requirements Documents (PRDs):** Link user stories and tasks to specific requirements.
- **Meeting Notes:** Reference action items or bug tickets discussed in sprint reviews or standups.
- **Project Plans:** Embed relevant epics, tasks, and timelines directly into planning pages.
- **Sprint Retrospectives:** Highlight completed or blocked tasks using linked issue reports.
- **Release Documentation:** Connect change logs and QA issues to post-release notes.

Methods for Linking Jira Issues in Confluence

There are several methods to create effective links between Jira and Confluence content. Each has its strengths, depending on the depth of visibility you want to offer.

1. Jira Issue Macros (Dynamic Linking)

The most powerful and commonly used method is the **Jira Issue Macro**, which allows you to embed live Jira issues directly into a Confluence page.

How to use it:

1. In your Confluence page, click the **Insert (+)** icon and select **Jira**.
2. Enter the issue key (e.g., JIRA-102) or search by filter.
3. Choose a display format: *table, list, single issue*, or *count*.
4. Insert the macro.

Benefits:

- Displays real-time issue status, priority, and assignee
- Enables hover previews for quick insight
- Automatically updates as issues change in Jira

2. Smart Links (Inline URLs)

You can also paste a Jira issue URL directly into a Confluence page. Confluence will automatically convert it into a **smart link preview**.

How to use it:

1. Copy a Jira issue link (e.g., https://yourdomain.atlassian.net/browse/PROJ-123)
2. Paste it into Confluence
3. Choose between *inline link, card,* or *embed view*

Benefits:

- Simple and fast
- Requires no macros or configuration
- Great for quick references in notes or discussions

3. Confluence Page Links Inside Jira

Linking works both ways. You can also add a **Confluence page link inside a Jira issue** to provide relevant documentation.

How to use it:

1. Open a Jira issue
2. Use the **"Link"** option in the issue menu
3. Select **Web Link** or **Confluence Page**
4. Paste the URL and give it a label

Benefits:

- Keeps important context within the Jira interface
- Encourages developers and task owners to review supporting documentation

---

Best Practices for Linking

To get the most out of Jira-Confluence linking, follow these guidelines:

- **Standardize naming conventions** for pages and issues so links are easily identifiable
- **Group related issues** using saved filters and embed them with the *Jira Filter* macro
- **Use Confluence templates** that include pre-inserted Jira macros for PRDs, meeting notes, or sprint plans
- **Avoid duplicate linking**—centralize where possible to keep content clean and navigable
- **Add labels and tags** to pages for better searchability when cross-referenced in Jira

---

Example Workflow: Linking PRDs to Jira Stories

Let's walk through a typical use case:

1. A product manager creates a **Product Requirements Document** in Confluence.
2. Within the document, they list each feature or requirement.
3. For each requirement, they insert a **Jira Issue Macro** linking to the related story or epic in Jira.
4. Developers working in Jira can now click through to the detailed documentation.
5. As Jira statuses update (e.g., In Progress, Done), the PRD in Confluence **reflects those updates in real time**.

This workflow enhances traceability, accountability, and alignment across the product lifecycle.

Summary

Linking Jira issues to Confluence pages is one of the most immediate and impactful steps toward **seamless collaboration**. It reduces silos, eliminates manual updates, and creates a unified view of both project intent and progress.

Embedding Jira Boards in Confluence

Bringing Work Visualization into Your Documentation Space

While linking Jira issues to Confluence pages is powerful, embedding entire **Jira boards** takes visibility and collaboration to a whole new level. By placing interactive Scrum or Kanban boards directly within Confluence, teams gain **real-time insight** into workflows—without toggling between tools. This chapter focuses on how to embed Jira boards in Confluence effectively, and why doing so can dramatically improve transparency, accountability, and team alignment.

Why Embed Jira Boards?

Embedding Jira boards into Confluence delivers several strategic benefits:

- **Live updates**: Any changes made in Jira are instantly reflected in Confluence.
- **Unified communication**: Discuss work and display task progress in the same space.
- **Stakeholder visibility**: Non-technical users can monitor progress without navigating Jira.
- **Contextual collaboration**: Combine planning notes, decisions, and boards on a single page.

In essence, embedding boards eliminates tool-switching and centralizes the project narrative.

Use Cases for Embedded Boards

- **Project Status Dashboards**: Show live sprint boards on a Confluence homepage or executive report.
- **Sprint Planning Documents**: Combine sprint goals, velocity targets, and the active sprint board.
- **Team Homepages**: Display current WIP and backlog status within each team's Confluence space.
- **Cross-Project Summaries**: Visualize multiple boards on a single page for program-level tracking.
- **Retrospective Reviews**: Reflect on completed sprints using the board's historical data.

How to Embed a Jira Board in Confluence

There are two primary methods to embed boards: **Jira Board Macros** and **Smart Links**.

1. Using the Jira Board Macro (Preferred Method)

Steps:

1. In your Confluence page, click **Insert (+)** and select **Jira**.
2. Choose **Search for issues**, or paste a **JQL query** that represents your board.
   - Example JQL: `project = "XYZ" ORDER BY Rank ASC`
3. Select **Display Options** and choose **Table**, **List**, or **Board View** (depending on your Jira plan).
4. Insert the macro.

Note: While board-style views are not always available natively, some advanced views require **Jira Software Premium** or plugins.

Benefits:

- Interactive view of issues

- Customizable columns and filters
- Automatically updates as Jira data changes

2. Using Smart Links (Quick View Option)

Steps:

1. Copy the URL of your Jira board from the Jira interface.
2. Paste the URL into a Confluence page.
3. Confluence will detect it as a smart link—select "**Embed view**" from the preview options.

Benefits:

- Extremely fast setup
- Retains interactive link to the full board
- Ideal for lightweight visibility needs

Limitations:

- Not as customizable as macros
- Displays a static visual or clickable card

Tips for Effective Board Embedding

- **Use space landing pages** to embed a team's current sprint or Kanban board.
- **Combine boards with status reports** and commentary for leadership updates.
- **Apply filters in your JQL** to focus on specific priorities (e.g., only "In Progress" items).
- **Label embedded boards clearly** with headings like "Development Sprint - Q2" or "UX Tasks This Week."
- **Avoid cluttering pages** with too many boards—limit to one or two per view for clarity.

Embedding vs. Linking: When to Use Each

Use Case	Recommended Method
Detailed tracking of individual issues	**Link Jira issues via macros**
Real-time task visualization	**Embed full Jira board**
Highlight one or two important tasks	**Use smart link previews**
Planning sessions with evolving goals	**Combine boards with documentation**
High-level stakeholder summaries	**Embed board in a Confluence dashboard page**

Example: Sprint Planning Page with Embedded Board

Let's consider a practical example:

Page Title: *Sprint 12 Planning – Team Alpha*

Page Content:

- Sprint Goals

- Velocity Capacity
- Key Stories and Dependencies
- Action Items from Previous Sprint
- **Embedded Jira Board:** *Team Alpha Sprint Board*
- Comments Section for Pre-Sprint Discussion

This format keeps everyone aligned on both the **narrative and execution** in a single, easily accessible space.

Summary

Embedding Jira boards in Confluence transforms static documentation into a **live project dashboard**. It brings workflows to life, improves cross-functional visibility, and fosters real-time collaboration. Whether you're planning, reporting, or reviewing, embedded boards provide the clearest window into team progress.

Syncing User Permissions Across Platforms

Ensuring Secure, Seamless Access Across Jira and Confluence

One of the most overlooked—but critical—components of successful integration between Jira and Confluence is **user permission management**. Without synchronized and well-configured permissions, your team may face access barriers, confusion over visibility, or even data security risks. Syncing user permissions ensures that team members have **consistent access rights**, promoting a smooth, secure, and collaborative user experience.

In this chapter, we'll explore the principles of permission alignment, best practices for syncing user access, and how to set up and maintain proper visibility across both platforms.

Why Syncing Permissions Matters

When Jira and Confluence are integrated but **permission schemes are not aligned**, users may:

- See broken links or inaccessible content
- Miss critical Jira issues or Confluence documentation
- Experience inconsistent collaboration capabilities (e.g., view-only access in one tool, full edit rights in another)
- Violate organizational security or compliance policies

A unified permission strategy avoids these pitfalls by providing a **cohesive experience** across platforms.

Understanding Permission Structures

Jira Permissions

Jira permissions are managed at **two levels**:

1. **Global Permissions** – Control access to the entire Jira instance (e.g., administrators, user access).
2. **Project Permissions** – Define what users can do within individual projects (e.g., browse, edit issues, assign tasks).

Jira uses **permission schemes**, **roles**, and **groups** to manage access.

Confluence Permissions

Confluence also manages permissions at **two levels**:

1. **Global Permissions** – Determine who can access the Confluence site and create spaces.
2. **Space Permissions** – Control what users can do within each space (e.g., view, edit, add pages, administer).

Like Jira, Confluence uses **groups** and **space permissions** for configuration.

Steps to Sync Permissions Across Platforms

1. Centralize User Management with Atlassian Admin

If you're using Jira and Confluence Cloud, both tools can be centrally managed via **Atlassian Admin**. This enables:

- Single user directory across both platforms
- Centralized group and role assignments
- Simplified billing and account control

For Server or Data Center editions, consider using **LDAP/Active Directory** or **Crowd** for centralized access control.

2. Create Shared Groups Across Jira and Confluence

Use common user groups (e.g., `dev-team`, `qa-team`, `product-managers`) and assign those groups matching roles in both Jira and Confluence.

Example:

- `dev-team` in Jira: Browse Projects, Transition Issues, Comment
- `dev-team` in Confluence: View Spaces, Edit Pages, Add Comments

This ensures that a developer logging into either system sees only what's relevant and is empowered to collaborate fully.

3. Use Roles to Manage Permissions Granularly

Both tools support **roles** (e.g., Developer, Project Lead, Space Admin). Assign users to roles at the project/space level to define what actions they can perform.

Benefits of roles:

- Simplifies permission updates
- Avoids direct user-by-user assignments
- Enhances security by limiting unnecessary access

4. Align Space and Project Ownership

For every Confluence space linked to a Jira project, assign **coordinated ownership**:

- A project admin in Jira should also be a space admin in Confluence
- This ensures updates to documentation and workflows are coordinated

Consistency in ownership improves accountability and governance.

Common Scenarios and How to Handle Them

Scenario	Recommended Action
User can view Jira tasks but not Confluence docs	Add the user to the proper Confluence space group or grant them view permission
Stakeholder should only view dashboards	Use read-only groups (e.g., `view-only`) in both platforms
Contractor needs temporary access	Create a `contractor` group with time-bound access limits

Team lead needs full editing rights in both tools	Assign to both Project Admin (Jira) and Space Admin (Confluence) roles

Permissions and Integration Features

To unlock **integration features**, such as embedding Jira content in Confluence or linking Confluence pages to Jira issues, users must have:

- Access to both platforms with the same Atlassian ID or synced account
- **Permission to view the linked content** (e.g., if a user sees a Confluence page with an embedded Jira macro, they must also have permission to view the Jira issue)

If a user lacks access on either side, embedded content will show as **"restricted" or "not found"**.

Best Practices for Ongoing Permission Management

- **Document your group and role strategy** as part of your onboarding process
- **Audit permissions quarterly** to identify inactive users or access gaps
- **Leverage automation or scripts** (especially with APIs) to maintain consistency across teams
- **Train admins** to understand both Jira and Confluence permission models
- **Use naming conventions** for groups to keep access organized (e.g., `jira-dev-read`, `conf-pm-write`)

Summary

Syncing user permissions across Jira and Confluence is vital for a seamless, secure collaboration experience. By aligning roles, standardizing group access, and managing users centrally, you eliminate roadblocks and ensure teams are empowered to work effectively across platforms.

Automating Updates Between Jira and Confluence

Eliminating Manual Effort, Enhancing Real-Time Collaboration

In an integrated environment, the ability to **automatically sync information** between Jira and Confluence saves time, reduces human error, and ensures that your documentation and task management are always up to date. By automating updates between these two platforms, teams can keep project stakeholders informed, maintain audit trails, and reduce the overhead of repetitive tasks.

This chapter explores the methods, tools, and best practices for automating updates between Jira and Confluence—creating a truly **dynamic, synchronized collaboration system**.

Why Automate?

Manual updates are not only time-consuming but also prone to being overlooked or outdated. Automation ensures:

- **Real-time visibility** into task progress and project health
- **Improved accuracy** of shared documentation
- **Consistent reporting** across stakeholders and departments
- **Fewer status meetings** and redundant communication
- **Better focus on strategic work** instead of administrative upkeep

Automation bridges the gap between planning (Confluence) and execution (Jira), making your workflows faster and smarter.

What Can Be Automated?

Here are the most common types of updates that can be automated between Jira and Confluence:

- **Updating Confluence pages when Jira issue statuses change**
- **Creating Jira issues from Confluence templates or checklists**
- **Auto-generating Confluence reports or meeting summaries based on Jira data**
- **Triggering Confluence page updates when sprint progress hits milestones**
- **Scheduling recurring reports (e.g., weekly status dashboards)**
- **Syncing comments or metadata across linked content**

Automation Tools and Methods

1. Jira Automation Rules

Jira Cloud includes a powerful **no-code automation engine**. You can use it to trigger actions based on issue events.

Example Use Case: "When an issue is transitioned to 'Done', append a summary comment to a linked Confluence page."

How to Set It Up:

1. Navigate to **Project Settings > Automation**

2. Click **Create Rule**
3. Choose a trigger (e.g., "Issue transitioned")
4. Add a condition (e.g., "Status = Done")
5. Add an action (e.g., "Send web request" to Confluence or "Link issue")
6. Test and publish the rule

Tip: Use the **"Send web request"** action to integrate with Confluence APIs if deeper customization is needed.

---

2. Confluence Page Macros with Dynamic Jira Data

Although not a traditional automation, using Jira macros within Confluence **dynamically pulls updated data** every time a page is loaded.

Examples:

- **Jira Filter Macro**: Auto-updates a list of open bugs, tasks, or stories
- **Jira Chart Macro**: Automatically refreshes graphs like burndown or velocity
- **Jira Roadmap Macro**: Shows live progress on larger initiatives

These macros act like live dashboards, reducing the need for manual data copying.

---

3. Third-Party Automation Apps

Atlassian Marketplace offers plugins that enhance automation between Jira and Confluence, including:

- **Elements Publish to Confluence**: Automatically creates Confluence pages from Jira data
- **Better Content Archiving**: Triggers actions based on content age and status
- **Automation Toolbox for Jira**: Adds more advanced triggers and actions
- **Scriptrunner** (Cloud or Data Center): Enables scripting custom automations

Best For: Teams with specialized needs or Server/Data Center instances where native automation is limited.

---

4. REST API Integration

For organizations with technical resources, both Jira and Confluence offer **robust REST APIs** to build custom automations.

Use Cases:

- Sync Jira comments to related Confluence pages
- Automatically update status sections in Confluence based on Jira transitions
- Push Confluence form inputs into Jira as issues or sub-tasks

Requires developer support but allows for unlimited customization and integration with other systems (e.g., Slack, Microsoft Teams, GitHub).

Best Practices for Automation

- **Start simple**: Automate high-impact, low-risk tasks first (e.g., daily report updates).
- **Use consistent naming conventions**: Helps identify linked content and automation rules.
- **Test in staging environments**: Especially for webhooks or API-based automation.
- **Maintain documentation**: Record all automation rules to avoid confusion across admins.
- **Monitor activity logs**: Jira and Confluence track automation events—use these to troubleshoot or optimize.

Example: Auto-Updating a Weekly Confluence Status Report

Workflow:

1. A Confluence page is created with the **Jira Filter Macro** pulling all issues in "In Progress" or "Done".
2. A Jira automation rule is set to **trigger weekly**, refreshing the filter and notifying the team via comment.
3. Confluence page also includes a **Jira Chart Macro** for real-time burndown tracking.

The result? A live, weekly status report that updates itself—no manual intervention required.

Summary

Automation is the key to making your Jira-Confluence integration **truly seamless and intelligent**. Whether you're using native rules, live macros, third-party tools, or custom scripts, automating updates removes friction and ensures that your team always works from the latest, most accurate data.

In the next section, we'll shift gears into **Practical Implementation**, where we'll guide you through a step-by-step setup to bring all these strategies to life in your own project environment.

Section 4:
Practical Implementation Steps

Step-by-Step Integration Setup Guide

Turning Strategy into Action

By now, you've learned the **why and what** of Jira-Confluence integration—now it's time for the **how**. This chapter provides a complete **step-by-step walkthrough** to connect Jira and Confluence, ensuring a functional and secure integration environment.

Whether you're using Atlassian Cloud or managing your own Data Center instances, this setup guide will help you establish the technical bridge that enables seamless collaboration between planning and execution.

Before You Begin: Pre-Integration Checklist

Ensure you've completed the following:

- **Jira and Confluence accounts created and active**
- **Admin access** to both platforms
- **Shared user directory or centralized identity management** (e.g., Atlassian Admin, LDAP)
- **Defined project-space mapping** (i.e., which Jira projects will link to which Confluence spaces)
- **Preliminary permission groups** established (e.g., developers, PMs, stakeholders)

With these in place, you're ready to integrate.

Step 1: Verify Product Access

For Atlassian Cloud:

1. Go to **admin.atlassian.com**
2. Ensure the same users or groups have access to both Jira and Confluence
3. Confirm your organization has both **Jira Software** and **Confluence** subscriptions active

For Server/Data Center:

1. Verify that both applications are running and accessible
2. Ensure **application links** are enabled in your server configuration
3. Confirm your license keys are valid and compatible with integration

Step 2: Establish Application Linking

Application Links (AppLinks) are the foundation for Jira-Confluence communication.

Atlassian Cloud (auto-linked):

1. Navigate to **Jira Settings > Applications > Application Links**
2. You should already see Confluence listed
3. If not, click **"Create link"**, enter your Confluence site URL, and follow the prompts

Jira Server/Data Center:

1. Go to **Jira Admin > Applications > Application Links**
2. Enter your Confluence base URL
3. Click **"Create new link"**
4. When prompted, **check the box** for reciprocal linking
5. Repeat the process from the Confluence admin panel to link Jira back
6. Authorize the connection using OAuth (recommended)

Note: Use the same protocol (http/https) across both tools to avoid connection errors.

Step 3: Enable Jira Macros in Confluence

To display Jira data inside Confluence:

1. In Confluence, go to **Settings > Application Links**
2. Click **Edit** next to your Jira link
3. Ensure OAuth (with impersonation) is enabled
4. Confirm that the **Jira Issues Macro**, **Jira Charts Macro**, and **Roadmap Macro** are activated under **Global Templates and Blueprints**

These macros allow live data to appear on Confluence pages using JQL, issue keys, or filters.

Step 4: Test Basic Integration Features

In Confluence:

- Create a new page
- Use the **Insert (+) > Jira** option
- Paste a Jira issue key (e.g., PROJ-101)
- Select the display format (table, list, single issue)
- Save and publish the page

In Jira:

- Open a Jira issue
- Use the **"More" (•••) > Link > Confluence Page**
- Paste a relevant Confluence page URL
- Save the link and verify bidirectional visibility

You should now see the issue linked in both platforms.

Step 5: Embed Live Reports and Dashboards

Enhance Confluence with live Jira data:

- **Jira Filter Macro**: Display issues from saved filters

- **Jira Chart Macro**: Add burndown charts, pie charts, or created/resolved graphs
- **Jira Roadmap Macro** (Premium): Visualize epics and project timelines

These reports update automatically with no need for manual refresh.

Step 6: Set Permissions for Integrated Content

Ensure users who view Confluence pages with embedded Jira content also have **permissions in Jira**:

- Grant appropriate **Browse Project** rights in Jira
- Verify **Space Permissions** in Confluence allow viewing or editing pages
- Use **shared groups** (e.g., project-contributors) to streamline access management

Without aligned permissions, users may see "restricted content" warnings or broken links.

Step 7: Activate Confluence Page Panels in Jira

To enable Confluence panels within Jira issues:

1. Go to **Jira Project Settings > Summary > Project Links**
2. Confirm the linked Confluence space
3. When viewing a Jira issue, scroll down to find the **"Confluence Pages"** panel
4. Users can now **create new pages from templates** or **link existing Confluence pages** directly from Jira

---

Step 8: Automate Workflows (Optional but Recommended)

Enable Jira automation to trigger updates in Confluence or vice versa:

- Go to **Jira Settings > System > Automation**
- Create a new rule (e.g., "When an issue transitions to Done, post an update to a linked Confluence page")
- Use **webhooks or APIs** for deeper automation

Confluence apps like *Elements Publish to Confluence* can also auto-generate documentation from Jira issue fields.

Troubleshooting Tips

Issue	Solution
Confluence page shows "No Jira Issues Found"	Check if the user has permission to view the Jira project
Application link not working	Ensure both tools use the same base protocol (HTTP/HTTPS)
Macro not rendering live data	Confirm JQL syntax is correct and filter is shared

"Not authorized" error when viewing embedded data	Align group and role permissions across platforms

Summary

A successful Jira-Confluence integration starts with a solid technical foundation: application links, permissions, macros, and basic user training. Once in place, you unlock a powerful collaborative ecosystem where **workflows are transparent, documentation is dynamic, and teams stay aligned.**

Creating Jira-Driven Confluence Templates

Standardizing Documentation with Dynamic Integration

One of the most powerful ways to streamline collaboration between Jira and Confluence is through the use of **Jira-driven templates** in Confluence. These templates act as dynamic, reusable blueprints that **automatically pull in Jira data**, enabling teams to create consistent, informative documentation—without duplicating effort.

In this chapter, you'll learn how to create and use Confluence templates that are not only structured and repeatable, but also **live-linked to Jira** for real-time updates. These templates are ideal for product requirements, sprint reviews, meeting notes, and project summaries.

Why Use Jira-Driven Templates?

Jira-powered Confluence templates offer several key benefits:

- **Standardization**: Ensure documentation across teams follows a consistent structure
- **Automation**: Eliminate manual updates by embedding live Jira data
- **Efficiency**: Save time with pre-built layouts and macros
- **Clarity**: Provide a unified view of tasks, progress, and context
- **Scalability**: Easily replicate for every sprint, project, or product release

Common Use Cases for Jira-Integrated Templates

- **Product Requirement Documents (PRDs)**
- **Sprint Planning Pages**
- **Retrospective Reports**
- **Release Notes**
- **QA Test Summaries**
- **Project Status Updates**

Step-by-Step: Creating a Jira-Driven Confluence Template

Step 1: Plan Your Template Structure

Before jumping into creation, outline what your template should include. A typical structure might look like:

- Title
- Purpose or Objective
- Linked Jira Epics or Stories
- Jira Progress Chart
- Discussion or Decisions
- Action Items

Tip: Use headings, tables, and callouts to maintain clarity and guide users through the content.

Step 2: Create a New Template in Confluence

1. Go to **Confluence Settings > Global Templates and Blueprints** (admin access required)
2. Click **Add New Template**
3. Name your template (e.g., "Product Requirement Document with Jira")
4. Click **Create**

Alternatively, create a **space-level template** by going to **Space Settings > Content Tools > Templates**

Step 3: Insert Jira Macros for Live Data

Within the template editor:

1. Click **Insert (+) > Jira**
2. Use the **Jira Issues Macro** to embed a JQL query like:
   - `project = XYZ AND fixVersion = "Next Release"`
   - `assignee = currentUser() AND status != Done`
3. Set the **Display Options** (table, list, count, single issue, etc.)

You can also insert:

- **Jira Charts Macro** to show issue progress, sprint burn-down, or created vs resolved
- **Jira Roadmap Macro** (Premium) for epic timelines
- **Jira Filter Result Macro** to show saved filters from Jira

These dynamic elements ensure the template always shows **up-to-date task data**.

Step 4: Add Smart Instructional Placeholders

Use placeholders and instructional text so users know what to replace when using the template:

- Example:

  <Insert Feature Description Here>
  <Paste Link to Related Epic or Story>
  <Update Acceptance Criteria Below>

This makes templates user-friendly, especially for cross-functional teams.

Step 5: Save and Publish the Template

Once the layout and macros are in place:

1. Click **Save**
2. Your template will now be available in the **"Create"** dialog when starting a new page
3. Users can select it from the list and begin customizing with specific project or sprint data

---

Bonus: Use Templates with Confluence Blueprints

If your template is used frequently, consider converting it into a **Confluence Blueprint** with additional automation such as:

- **Auto-populated page titles** (e.g., "Sprint Review – Week [Date]")
- **Pre-linked Jira filters** based on the current project context
- **Custom page metadata** for tracking version or department

This requires more advanced setup using [Atlassian's SDK or marketplace apps] (https://developer.atlassian.com/), but it offers powerful automation for enterprise use.

Best Practices for Template Design

- **Keep it modular**: Use sections so teams can update only what's needed
- **Avoid overcomplication**: Don't include every macro—focus on relevance
- **Use labels**: Automatically categorize pages created from your templates
- **Document template usage**: Include a short guide on when and how to use it
- **Review and update templates periodically** to reflect process changes

---

Example: Sprint Planning Template with Jira Integration

Page Title: *Sprint Planning – Week [Date]*

Template Content:

- **Goals for This Sprint**: *Insert goals here*
- **Jira Stories to be Delivered**: *Jira Issues Macro:* `project = DEV AND sprint in openSprints()`
- **Sprint Burndown Chart**: *Jira Chart Macro*
- **Team Notes and Risks**: *Insert comments*
- **Action Items**: *Insert checklist*

This setup ensures sprint planning is visible, measurable, and repeatable.

Summary

Jira-driven Confluence templates are a game-changer for **standardizing documentation** while keeping it **live and interactive**. By embedding dynamic Jira content directly into your templates, you eliminate redundant work, improve cross-team collaboration, and create documentation that evolves with your projects.

Using Macros for Dynamic Content Sharing

Making Confluence Content Live, Interactive, and Always Up-to-Date

One of Confluence's most powerful features—especially when integrated with Jira—is its support for **macros**. Macros allow you to transform ordinary Confluence pages into **dynamic, data-driven, and interactive workspaces**. When combined with Jira, macros enable teams to visualize live task data, progress charts, reports, and much more—without ever leaving the Confluence interface.

This chapter explores how to leverage Confluence macros to share Jira content dynamically, streamline collaboration, and eliminate the need for manual updates in your documentation.

What Are Macros?

Macros are smart components that add dynamic or advanced functionality to Confluence pages. You can use them to:

- Embed Jira issues, filters, and reports
- Display live project metrics and charts
- Collapse/expand content for cleaner layouts
- Create buttons, tabs, and panels
- Pull external or internal data into your pages

When used properly, macros **bring your pages to life**—turning them from static documents into evolving dashboards and real-time status reports.

Key Jira-Related Macros in Confluence

Below are the essential macros to use when integrating Jira data into Confluence:

1. Jira Issues Macro

Purpose: Display a list, table, or summary of Jira issues based on JQL or filter ID.

Usage:

- Insert via **Insert (+) > Jira**
- Input JQL like `project = ABC AND status != Done`
- Customize columns (e.g., Key, Summary, Assignee, Status)
- Choose display format (table, list, count, or single issue)

Use Cases:

- Team dashboards
- Bug tracking summaries
- Feature roll-up reports

2. Jira Charts Macro

Purpose: Visualize Jira data in the form of charts.

Types Available:

- Pie Chart
- Created vs. Resolved Chart
- Average Age Chart
- Time Since Chart
- Workload Pie Chart

Usage:

- Insert via **Insert > Other Macros > Jira Chart**
- Choose a saved filter or JQL
- Define chart type and time frame

Use Cases:

- Burndown or burnup visualizations
- Progress breakdowns by status, priority, or assignee
- Sprint health snapshots

---

3. Jira Roadmap Macro (Premium Feature)

Purpose: Display an interactive timeline of Jira epics across teams or projects.

Use Cases:

- High-level project tracking
- Visual roadmaps for product stakeholders
- Timeline views for cross-team initiatives

---

4. Jira Filter Results Macro

Purpose: Embed the results of a saved Jira filter directly into a page.

Benefits:

- Easy to maintain—update the filter once and it's reflected on all pages
- Ideal for standardized reports and dashboards

Tip: Use shared filters across projects to maintain consistency.

Enhancing Your Macros with Layout and Design

Pair macros with other Confluence formatting options to **maximize clarity and usability**:

- Use **Section and Column macros** to create responsive layouts
- Add **Expand macros** to hide long issue lists or definitions until needed
- Include **Info, Warning, or Note macros** to emphasize important updates or changes
- Combine multiple macros on the same page for unified dashboards (e.g., charts + filter + page tree)

Practical Examples of Dynamic Macro Use

Weekly Team Report Page

- **Title**: *Team Velocity & Issue Summary – Week of [Date]*
- **Content**:
    - Jira Chart Macro (Velocity)
    - Jira Issues Macro (In Progress Tasks)
    - Jira Issues Macro (Bugs Closed This Week)
    - Expand Macro (for retrospective notes)

Sprint Planning Page

- **Title**: *Sprint Planning – Sprint 14*
- **Content**:
    - Sprint Goal (plain text)
    - Jira Filter Results Macro (Open Stories in Backlog)
    - Jira Pie Chart Macro (Work by Priority)
    - Jira Roadmap Macro (Epics Timeline)

Tips for Using Macros Effectively

- **Name saved filters clearly**: This ensures team members know what data is being pulled
- **Use page labels and metadata**: Helps with searchability and automated reporting
- **Train your team**: Show non-technical users how to use macros to consume live Jira data
- **Avoid information overload**: Only embed relevant issues or charts—too many macros can clutter a page
- **Test permissions**: Ensure all users have access to the Jira data shown in Confluence, or they'll see "No issues found" errors

---

Automating Macro Updates

Remember: once you embed Jira data via macros, it **automatically stays up to date**. Any change in Jira—new issue creation, status transitions, or reassignments—will reflect instantly in Confluence pages using those macros. No manual refresh or maintenance required.

You can also schedule recurring emails or Slack updates with links to macro-driven Confluence pages to **replace static reports**.

Summary

Macros are the cornerstone of **dynamic content sharing** in Confluence. By embedding live Jira data using issue lists, charts, and filters, you create powerful, real-time documentation that adapts to your team's work. These macros save time, reduce duplication, and offer greater visibility across all levels of your organization.

Configuring Notifications and Alerts

Keeping Everyone Informed Without Overload

A seamless Jira-Confluence integration isn't just about data syncing—it's about **ensuring the right people are notified at the right time**. Effective notifications and alerts help teams stay aligned, prevent delays, and respond quickly to updates. But poorly configured alerts can cause noise and fatigue, leading users to ignore important changes.

This chapter focuses on how to configure **targeted, actionable, and manageable notifications** across Jira and Confluence to enhance visibility, accountability, and responsiveness without overwhelming your team.

The Role of Notifications in Integrated Collaboration

When set up thoughtfully, notifications can:

- **Promote accountability** by alerting users of task assignments or due dates
- **Speed up workflows** by informing stakeholders of key changes
- **Support transparency** across cross-functional teams
- **Reduce meetings and manual status checks** by automating updates

Your goal is to **balance awareness with relevance**.

Notification Sources in Jira and Confluence

Here's a breakdown of where notifications come from:

Jira

- **Email notifications** based on issue activity
- **@mentions** in comments or descriptions
- **Automation rules** that send custom emails or Slack messages
- **Watchers** added to specific issues or projects
- **Notifications for boards, filters, and dashboards**

Confluence

- **Page watches** (users watch pages, spaces, or blogs)
- **@mentions** in page comments or content
- **Notifications on page edits or comments**
- **Daily digest emails**
- **Third-party integrations** (e.g., Slack, Teams)

Step-by-Step: Configuring Notifications in Jira

1. Customize the Notification Scheme

1. Go to **Jira Settings > Issues > Notification Schemes**
2. Choose or create a scheme that matches your project needs
3. Define who gets notified for each event (e.g., Issue Created, Updated, Resolved)

Assign roles like Reporter, Assignee, Project Lead, or a specific group

2. Use @Mentions for Direct Attention

Encourage your team to use **@mentions** in issue comments and descriptions. This triggers instant alerts to specific users without altering the global notification scheme.

3. Add Watchers for Key Stakeholders

Anyone added as a **watcher** will receive notifications about changes and comments on that issue.

4. Create Automation Rules for Alerts

Navigate to **Project Settings > Automation**:

- Create a rule like: "When priority = Critical AND status = In Progress, then send an email to DevOps team."
- Or: "When an issue is moved to Done, then post a message to the #qa-review Slack channel."

You can also use **Slack, Microsoft Teams, or webhook integrations** for real-time, cross-platform alerts.

Step-by-Step: Configuring Notifications in Confluence

1. Control Watch Settings

Users can:

- Watch individual pages
- Watch entire spaces
- Manage notification frequency under **Profile > Settings > Email**

Encourage users to watch only what's relevant to avoid overload.

2. Use @Mentions in Comments and Pages

@Mentioning a teammate in a comment or body of a page triggers a direct notification and draws attention to specific content needing review or input.

3. Set Up Page or Space Watches for Teams

For team pages (e.g., Sprint Planning, Weekly Reports), have contributors or stakeholders watch the page or space to stay notified of updates or changes.

4. Use Third-Party Notification Enhancements

Tools like:

- **Slack for Confluence**
- **Microsoft Teams for Confluence**
- **Better Content Archiving** (automated reminders and content status updates) can push targeted alerts to communication platforms your team already uses.

Best Practices for Notification Management

- **Avoid notification overload**: Remove unnecessary watchers or reduce frequency for general updates.
- **Segment alerts by role**: Only notify users when the update directly impacts their work.
- **Encourage personal customization**: Let users manage their own notification settings.
- **Use automated summaries**: Replace manual check-ins with automated status digest pages or emails.
- **Include alert guidelines in onboarding**: Educate new users on how to manage their alerts effectively.

Example: Automating a Weekly Status Alert via Confluence + Jira

Workflow:

1. A Confluence page titled *Weekly Status Dashboard* pulls live data using Jira macros.
2. Every Friday at 10 AM, a Jira automation rule triggers a **Slack message** or **email** to stakeholders:
   - "Your weekly project dashboard is ready. [View it here]"
3. Confluence sends a page edit notification if the dashboard is manually updated.

This workflow reduces the need for status meetings while keeping everyone informed in real-time.

Summary

Properly configured notifications and alerts ensure your integrated Jira-Confluence environment delivers **just-in-time information without excessive noise**. Whether through native settings, automation, or third-party tools, alerts should help your team act quickly and stay aligned—without becoming a distraction.

Migrating Legacy Data to the Integrated System

Bringing Historical Knowledge into Your Unified Workflow

To fully leverage the power of a Jira-Confluence integration, you need more than just a clean setup—you need your historical data. Past Jira issues, Confluence documents, spreadsheets, and even emails often hold essential knowledge, decisions, and context that shouldn't be left behind. Migrating this **legacy data** into your new integrated environment ensures that your team retains valuable insights while working from a single source of truth.

This chapter walks you through how to **identify, prepare, and migrate** legacy data into Jira and Confluence, ensuring continuity, clarity, and collaboration from day one.

Why Migrate Legacy Data?

Migration can feel like a chore—but its benefits are strategic:

- **Preserves decision history** and project rationale
- **Avoids duplication of work** already completed
- **Enables smarter planning** with historical insights
- **Simplifies onboarding** for new team members
- **Centralizes documentation** for faster search and reference

In short, good migration ensures your new system doesn't start from scratch—it starts smart.

Step 1: Identify What Should Be Migrated

Not all data is worth migrating. Focus on information that is:

- **Still relevant** to ongoing work or reference
- **Legally or contractually required** to keep
- **Frequently accessed** by team members
- **Crucial for audits or compliance**
- **Useful for historical trend analysis** (e.g., velocity, defects, releases)

Common legacy data sources include:

- Old Jira projects or alternative ticketing systems
- Confluence archives or wiki tools
- Spreadsheets, Google Docs, and PDFs
- Email threads with task-related decisions
- Shared drives or file servers

Step 2: Define Your Migration Strategy

Choose an approach based on the volume and type of data.

Strategy	Best For	Tools

Manual Migration	Small volumes of content	Copy-paste, file upload, Jira issue creation
Bulk Import	Structured data (e.g., CSV, XML)	Jira CSV Importer, Confluence Page Importer
API-Based Migration	Large, automated migrations	Atlassian REST APIs
Third-Party Tools	Complex or cross-system imports	Tools like *Project Configurator, Xporter, ScriptRunner*

For Confluence, you can also **import entire spaces** using space export/import features.

Step 3: Prepare Jira Data for Import

If you're importing issues from a legacy system:

1. Export the issues into **CSV** format
2. Ensure columns are correctly labeled: Summary, Description, Assignee, Priority, Status, etc.
3. Map your custom fields in Jira to match the CSV columns
4. In Jira, go to **System > External System Import > CSV**
5. Upload and map fields to your Jira configuration
6. Validate the import and perform a test run

Tip: Group historical issues into archived projects or mark them with a "Legacy" label to avoid cluttering active boards.

Step 4: Prepare Confluence Data for Import

To bring in documentation:

Option 1: Manual Page Creation

- Copy content from old docs into new Confluence pages
- Use Jira macros to link newly imported Jira issues

Option 2: Bulk Upload or Import

- Upload multiple files using the "Files & Images" tool
- Use the **Confluence Word or PDF importer** for single documents
- For entire spaces:
  - Go to **Confluence Admin > Backup & Restore**
  - Import a previously exported XML space file

Option 3: REST API Automation

- Use Confluence's REST API to bulk create pages with embedded Jira links

---

Step 5: Re-link Legacy Data Across Jira and Confluence

Once your data is in place, **establish relationships** between imported content:

- Use the **Jira Issues macro** on Confluence pages to show linked legacy issues
- Add Confluence page links into related Jira issues via the "Link" field
- Create **index pages** in Confluence for older documentation grouped by topic, project, or date

This preserves traceability and makes it easier for teams to find relevant historical context.

Step 6: Archive What You Don't Migrate

Some data should not be imported, but still needs to be stored for compliance or reference.

- Use **Confluence archive spaces** or dedicated "Legacy" pages
- Use **Jira archived projects** or statuses (e.g., "Obsolete")
- Maintain a separate **read-only file repository** for static historical files

Label archived content clearly and communicate how team members can access it if needed.

Step 7: Validate and Communicate

Before going live with your integrated system:

- Test access to imported Jira issues and Confluence pages
- Check that macros and links work properly
- Review permissions to ensure only authorized users can view sensitive content
- Notify the team about what was migrated and where it lives
- Provide a guide or index for navigating imported content

Example: Migrating a Legacy Product Requirement Document

1. Export the old PRD from Google Docs as a Word file
2. Import it into Confluence using the Word Importer
3. Create a new Jira epic to represent the project
4. Link related historical Jira tickets using the **Jira Issues Macro**
5. Add a Confluence label: `legacy-prd`
6. Update the page with current project context at the top

This ensures the old PRD remains accessible and searchable—without interfering with current workflows.

Summary

Migrating legacy data is a crucial step in building a fully integrated Jira-Confluence system. With thoughtful selection, structured imports, and proper linking, your new environment will retain the knowledge of your past—while positioning your team for better, faster collaboration in the future.

Section 5:
Enhancing Collaboration Workflows

Streamlining Sprint Planning with Jira and Confluence

Aligning Strategy, Execution, and Team Collaboration

Sprint planning is one of the most critical rituals in Agile teams. It defines the work for the coming sprint, aligns team members, and sets a clear direction for what success looks like. By integrating Jira and Confluence, teams can transform this planning process from a fragmented meeting into a **seamless, data-driven collaboration experience**.

In this chapter, you'll learn how to use Jira and Confluence together to **streamline sprint planning**, minimize manual preparation, and ensure everyone enters the sprint fully aligned and ready to deliver.

The Challenge with Traditional Sprint Planning

Sprint planning often suffers from:

- Scattered documentation across tools or emails
- Repetitive preparation for every sprint
- Lack of historical reference for previous sprints
- Difficulty visualizing the link between goals and deliverables
- Unclear ownership or misalignment on priorities

Jira and Confluence, when used in tandem, address these issues by centralizing tasks, discussions, goals, and performance insights—all in one integrated flow.

Key Benefits of Integrating Jira and Confluence for Sprint Planning

- **Link goals to execution**: Define sprint goals in Confluence and link them directly to Jira stories.
- **Live visibility**: Use Jira macros to pull in real-time issue updates into your planning page.
- **Standardized templates**: Create repeatable Confluence templates for every planning session.
- **Collaborative pre-work**: Let team members review, comment, and contribute asynchronously.
- **Data-driven decisions**: Leverage Jira velocity charts and burndown insights for better planning.

Recommended Sprint Planning Workflow

Here's how you can streamline your sprint planning using Jira and Confluence together:

Step 1: Use a Sprint Planning Confluence Template

Start with a standardized Confluence page template for sprint planning. A strong template typically includes:

- Sprint Name and Dates
- Sprint Goal (strategic objective)
- Jira Filter for Selected Stories
- Jira Chart showing velocity or workload
- Links to retrospectives or previous sprints
- Discussion/Comments section
- Action items from the meeting

Example macro usage:

- `Jira Issues Macro` for sprint backlog
- `Jira Chart Macro` for velocity history
- `Expand Macros` for comments or risks

Step 2: Pull in Jira Data with Macros

Use dynamic macros to avoid manual copy-pasting:

- **JQL Example**: `project = WEB AND sprint in openSprints() AND issuetype in (Story, Bug)`
- **Display format**: Table view with columns like Summary, Assignee, Status, Story Points
- Add a **Jira Pie Chart** to visualize workload by assignee or issue type

This ensures that your Confluence page **automatically updates** as Jira issues are created or modified.

Step 3: Link Planning Content to Jira Stories

On each story or epic in Jira, link back to the Confluence planning page:

- Open Jira issue > More (•••) > **Link** > **Confluence Page**
- Choose "relates to" or "documents"

This helps product owners, developers, and stakeholders trace the **"why" behind each ticket**, reducing confusion and unnecessary meetings later.

Step 4: Collaborate in Confluence Before the Meeting

Encourage the team to engage in **pre-sprint discussions** on the Confluence page:

- Use @mentions to assign preparation tasks
- Add comments on proposed stories or concerns
- Identify blockers or dependencies ahead of time

This asynchronous preparation allows for **shorter, more focused planning meetings**.

Step 5: Run the Sprint Planning Meeting

During the live planning session:

- Use the Confluence page as your **shared agenda and reference**
- Review the sprint goal and priority stories together
- Update story estimates directly in Jira
- Document decisions and action items live in Confluence

The result is a **single page that captures your entire sprint planning context and commitment**.

Step 6: Post-Planning Follow-Up

Once the planning session is complete:

- Mark the Confluence page as "Sprint Planning – Finalized"
- Add page labels like `sprint-24`, `planning`, or `q2-release` for easy search
- Share the page link in Slack or Teams with a summary for transparency
- Use Confluence watch or automation to notify relevant stakeholders

---

Bonus Tip: Connect the Sprint Planning Page to the Sprint Retrospective

Link each sprint planning page to its corresponding **retrospective** using the `related pages` feature or a "Previous Sprint" section.

This allows teams to continuously **reflect on what was planned versus what was delivered**, improving each iteration over time.

Summary

By streamlining sprint planning with Jira and Confluence, teams shift from scattered and redundant planning to a **centralized, repeatable, and transparent** process. Real-time Jira data embedded in collaborative Confluence pages ensures that planning is rooted in reality, aligned with business goals, and accessible to all stakeholders.

Real-Time Documentation During Development

Keeping Knowledge and Code in Sync with Integrated Workflows

In traditional development environments, documentation often trails behind code—updated sporadically, written hastily after project delivery, or worse, abandoned altogether. This disconnect can lead to miscommunication, delays, and costly rework. However, by integrating Jira with Confluence and fostering a culture of **real-time documentation**, teams can ensure that project insights, technical decisions, and progress updates evolve alongside development itself.

This chapter explores how to use Jira and Confluence together to establish a workflow where documentation is **not an afterthought**, but a **living, collaborative companion** to the development process.

Why Real-Time Documentation Matters

- **Prevents knowledge silos** and captures key decisions as they happen
- **Improves onboarding** by providing up-to-date context
- **Enables transparency** across technical and non-technical stakeholders
- **Supports Agile ceremonies** like daily standups and sprint reviews
- **Reduces errors** caused by outdated or missing documentation

Instead of viewing documentation as a separate phase, integrated teams **build it as they code**, making it part of their sprint rhythm.

Key Principles for Real-Time Documentation

1. **Documentation should live close to the work**
2. **Updates should be incremental and collaborative**
3. **Structure should support reusability and searchability**
4. **Jira and Confluence should dynamically reflect project progress**

With these principles, you can turn Confluence into a real-time project hub and Jira into the source of truth for actionable tasks.

Setting Up Your Real-Time Documentation Environment

1. Create a Confluence Space for Active Projects

- Organize it by project or team (e.g., "Web Team Active Projects")
- Use page hierarchies like:
  - Sprint 21
    - Daily Standups
    - Task Breakdown
    - Sprint Notes
  - Feature X
    - Requirements
    - Architecture Decisions
    - Linked Jira Epics

2. Link Jira Issues into Confluence Pages

Throughout development, embed Jira macros into Confluence pages:

- **Task Tracker**: Use `Jira Filter Macro` to show current sprint stories, bugs, or subtasks
- **Change Logs**: Automatically reflect updates by displaying "Done" issues for each sprint
- **Progress Boards**: Embed boards or issue lists filtered by assignee, label, or component

This creates real-time visibility into work as it's happening.

3. Document Key Events and Decisions As They Occur

- **Use Confluence during standups** to log blockers, task updates, and discussion notes
- **Create Architecture Decision Records (ADRs)** directly linked to Jira epics
- **Add retrospective insights** during the sprint rather than after

Encourage developers and PMs to treat documentation as **collaborative commentary**, not just formal reporting.

Recommended Real-Time Documentation Practices

Event	Documentation Action
Sprint Kickoff	Start a Confluence planning page with linked Jira stories and goals
Daily Standup	Use a running Confluence page for notes, blockers, and priorities
Feature Development	Maintain a live spec or technical note linked to the Jira epic
Bug Fix	Document root cause and resolution linked to the bug issue
Code Review	Summarize feedback and decisions in a Confluence page for future reference
Sprint Review	Use Jira data to auto-generate a summary of completed work

Tools That Enhance Real-Time Documentation

- **Jira Issues Macro**: Embed specific stories, tasks, or epics into any page
- **Jira Chart Macro**: Display sprint burndown or issue trends dynamically
- **@Mentions in Confluence**: Bring in team members to contribute or review
- **Task Lists in Confluence**: Create collaborative checklists linked to Jira issues
- **Labeling and Page Templates**: Standardize formats and enable easy filtering/search

Automating the Flow

- Use **Jira Automation** to comment on linked Confluence pages when an issue status changes
- Configure **daily Slack or email digests** linking to Confluence documentation updates
- Use **blueprints or page templates** that pre-load Jira macros and team checklists

This automation reduces the burden of manual updates and promotes regular engagement.

Example: Feature Development in Real Time

Scenario: A new login feature is under development.

Workflow:

1. **Confluence Page**: "Feature: Secure Login System"
   - Linked Jira epic
   - Description, requirements, mockups
   - Embedded Jira issues for tasks and bugs
2. **During Development**:
   - Developers log decisions on OAuth implementation
   - QA adds notes on edge-case scenarios
   - PM tracks progress via macro-fed Jira tables
3. **Outcome**:
   - A single evolving page captures everything from ideation to deployment
   - Reuse for future login-related enhancements

Summary

Real-time documentation transforms how teams communicate and collaborate. By embedding Jira into Confluence workflows and treating documentation as a continuous, team-wide responsibility, you create an environment where knowledge is **current, accessible, and aligned** with development itself.

Running Effective Meetings Using Shared Resources

Elevating Collaboration with Integrated Agendas, Actions, and Insights

Meetings are meant to align teams, solve problems, and accelerate progress. Yet, in many organizations, they devolve into time-consuming sessions with no clear outcomes or follow-through. By integrating Jira and Confluence, you can transform meetings into **efficient, purposeful, and trackable collaboration sessions**—where shared resources, live updates, and centralized documentation keep everyone focused and accountable.

This chapter explores how to run effective meetings—standups, sprint reviews, retrospectives, and stakeholder check-ins—by leveraging Jira and Confluence together.

The Problem with Traditional Meetings

Without the right structure and tools, meetings often suffer from:

- Lack of clear agendas and ownership
- Poor visibility into project status
- Manual note-taking and forgotten action items
- Disconnected follow-up from daily operations
- Repeated discussions due to missing documentation

Integrated platforms solve this by unifying content, context, and action—all in one place.

Benefits of Using Jira and Confluence for Meeting Management

- **Live visibility into tasks, blockers, and progress**
- **One-click access to linked issues and documents**
- **Standardized templates for recurring meeting types**
- **Action items tied to Jira tasks for accountability**
- **Shared pages that track meeting history and decisions**

With a few best practices, you can replace ineffective meetings with **agile, results-oriented discussions**.

Key Meeting Types and How to Optimize Them

1. Daily Standups

Objective: Share progress, identify blockers, and plan the day

Confluence Setup:

- Use a recurring page (e.g., "Daily Standup – Sprint 24")
- Sections: Yesterday / Today / Blockers
- Use @mentions to assign speaking order or topics
- Embed a `Jira Filter Macro` showing "In Progress" and "To Do" items

Jira Tip: Highlight items that changed status in the last 24 hours using JQL: `updated >= -1d AND sprint in openSprints()`

---

2. Sprint Reviews

Objective: Demonstrate completed work, gather feedback, and evaluate outcomes

Confluence Setup:

- Title: "Sprint Review – Sprint [Number]"
- Sections: Completed Issues, Demo Links, Stakeholder Feedback
- Embed a Jira Issues macro with filter: `project = XYZ AND sprint = currentSprint() AND status = Done`
- Add Jira Chart Macro to show velocity or completed vs. planned items

Action Item Tracking: Document stakeholder comments and turn them into Jira stories directly from the page using Smart Links.

---

3. Retrospectives

Objective: Reflect on the sprint, identify improvements, and agree on actions

Confluence Setup:

- Use a template with:
    - What went well
    - What didn't
    - What to improve
    - Action items
- Insert Jira issues for unresolved bugs, blockers, or technical debt
- Use voting macros or comments for team engagement

Jira Integration: Convert retro action items into Jira tasks and link them to the retrospective page.

---

4. Stakeholder or Project Status Meetings

Objective: Share project updates, risks, and roadmap milestones

Confluence Setup:

- Executive-friendly template with project summary, KPIs, timelines
- Use the **Jira Roadmap Macro** to visualize timelines
- Embed charts showing current bug trends, feature progress, or blockers
- Include a decision log section with page anchors for quick reference

Best Practice: Set page restrictions to control visibility and protect sensitive data.

How to Make Meetings Actionable

- Assign Jira tasks during the meeting using Smart Links

- Summarize the meeting at the top of the Confluence page
- Use Confluence **task lists** and link each item to the corresponding Jira issue
- Tag responsible team members with @mentions for immediate visibility
- Use the **Watch feature** to notify stakeholders when the meeting page is updated

---

Best Practices for Integrated Meeting Management

Practice	Description
Use reusable templates	Standardize meeting structure across teams
Embed Jira content	Replace static agendas with live status and data
Keep pages short and scannable	Use headings, bullets, and macros for clarity
Link every action item to Jira	Avoid tasks getting lost in notes
Review previous meeting notes before each session	Ensure continuity and accountability

---

Example: Running a Sprint Planning & Review Cycle

1. **Sprint Planning Page**
   - Sprint goal, Jira issues macro, estimation table
   - Created at the start of the sprint
2. **Daily Standup Pages**
   - Linked from planning page
   - Updated asynchronously or daily during the team check-in
3. **Sprint Review Page**
   - Pulls in completed issues via Jira macro
   - Includes demo links and feedback from product owners
4. **Retrospective Page**
   - Linked to the same sprint
   - Lists improvement tasks as Jira tickets

Together, this forms a **chain of living documentation** for that sprint—auditable, collaborative, and efficient.

Summary

Effective meetings aren't about talking more—they're about achieving clarity and driving results. With Confluence and Jira working together, you can create **agendas powered by real-time data, document outcomes in context, and turn ideas into action**—all within the same integrated workflow.

Building a Centralized Project Dashboard

Turning Data Into Visibility, Alignment, and Confidence

In a fast-paced, collaborative environment, project teams need a **single, up-to-date source of truth**—one that consolidates task progress, blockers, sprint health, and documentation into one accessible space. A centralized project dashboard is the answer. By integrating Jira and Confluence, you can create real-time dashboards that empower stakeholders, reduce status meetings, and drive better decisions through clear visibility.

This chapter will guide you through designing and building a powerful, centralized dashboard using Jira and Confluence together.

Why You Need a Centralized Dashboard

Without centralized visibility, teams often struggle with:

- Fragmented tools and siloed updates
- Manual status reporting and redundant meetings
- Unclear ownership or delivery timelines
- Delayed response to risks or dependencies
- Stakeholders constantly asking, "Where do we stand?"

A well-designed dashboard solves all of this by providing **automated, visual, and actionable status reporting.**

Characteristics of an Effective Dashboard

A great project dashboard is:

- **Live**: Automatically updates with real-time Jira data
- **Actionable**: Highlights blockers, upcoming deadlines, and ownership
- **Customized**: Tailored to the team, project phase, or stakeholder level
- **Accessible**: Easy to navigate and shared via a persistent link
- **Visual**: Uses charts, tables, and hierarchy to communicate clearly

---

Step 1: Identify Your Audience and Scope

Start by defining:

- **Who** the dashboard is for (e.g., product team, leadership, cross-functional squads)
- **What** it should cover (e.g., sprint progress, backlog status, QA metrics, delivery risks)
- **How often** it should be referenced (daily standups, weekly syncs, monthly reviews)

Example audience-specific dashboards:

- **Team Dashboards** – sprint goals, open issues, blockers
- **Manager Dashboards** – velocity, overdue tasks, resource load
- **Executive Dashboards** – roadmap view, high-level KPIs, major risks

---

Step 2: Set Up a Dedicated Confluence Page

Create a dedicated page or section in your project space called: **Project Dashboard – [Project Name]**

Structure it with clear headings and macros like:

- **Project Summary**
- **Sprint Progress (Jira Filter Macro)**
- **Issue Breakdown by Status (Jira Pie Chart)**
- **Open Bugs or Risks (JQL Filter)**
- **Upcoming Deadlines**
- **Related Documentation Links**
- **Owner & Stakeholder Info**

Use the **Table of Contents Macro** at the top for easy navigation.

Step 3: Embed Live Jira Data Using Macros

Recommended Jira Macros:

1. **Jira Issues Macro**
   - Filter: `project = PROJ AND sprint in openSprints() AND status not in (Done)`
   - Display as a table grouped by assignee or issue type
2. **Jira Chart Macro**
   - Pie Chart: Issue types or assignees
   - Created vs. Resolved: Sprint burn analysis
   - Average Age: How long tasks have been open
3. **Jira Roadmap Macro** (if using Jira Premium)
   - Display epics over time for roadmap visibility
4. **Jira Filter Result Macro**
   - Saved filters from Jira (e.g., `My team's unresolved bugs`)

These macros **auto-refresh**, meaning no manual updates are needed.

Step 4: Visualize and Highlight Key Metrics

Use formatting and visuals to draw attention to what matters:

- **Status Panels**: Use Confluence's Panel Macro to highlight blockers or delivery risks
- **Colored Labels or Emojis**: Indicate health (e.g., Green = On Track, Red = At Risk)
- **Decision Logs**: Use a table to track key approvals or project changes
- **Action Items Table**: List follow-ups and link them to Jira tickets via Smart Links

---

Step 5: Link Supporting Pages and Documents

The dashboard should serve as a **gateway** to deeper documentation:

- Sprint planning and retrospective pages
- Design or requirement documents

- Meeting notes
- Retrospective insights
- Technical specs or test plans

Use the **Page Properties and Page Properties Report Macros** to auto-summarize key details across sub-pages.

Step 6: Share and Maintain the Dashboard

Make your dashboard discoverable:

- Pin it to the top of the project space
- Add it to Slack or Teams channels
- Share the link in recurring calendar invites
- Encourage team members to bookmark it

Schedule a quick **weekly check** to validate the filters and ensure macros are rendering correctly. This keeps the dashboard relevant and trusted.

Example: Weekly Project Health Dashboard

Header: Project Alpha Dashboard – Week of [Date]

Sections:

- Project Summary (1-paragraph update)
- Active Sprint Overview (Jira Filter Macro)
- Sprint Velocity Chart (Jira Chart Macro)
- Blocked Issues (Jira Filter: `status = Blocked`)
- Bugs by Priority (Pie Chart Macro)
- Team Workload (Grouped Issue List)
- Links: Planning, Retro, Roadmap

Stakeholders can now access **everything they need in one page**, in under 2 minutes.

Summary

A centralized project dashboard is more than a report—it's a **real-time command center** for collaboration. With Jira fueling the data and Confluence providing the structure, your dashboard becomes the one place everyone trusts to track work, make decisions, and stay aligned.

In the next section, we'll dive into **advanced techniques for power users**, where you'll learn how to customize your workflows even further with scripts, APIs, and marketplace tools to extend your integration beyond the basics.

Section 6:
Advanced Techniques for Power Users

Custom Scripts and APIs for Deeper Integration

Supercharging Your Jira-Confluence Workflow with Automation and Code

While native integration between Jira and Confluence covers most collaboration needs, power users and developers often require **deeper, tailored functionality**—something not always achievable through built-in features or marketplace apps. That's where custom scripting and APIs come in.

This chapter introduces the use of **Jira and Confluence REST APIs**, **automation scripts**, and **third-party scripting tools** to enhance your project management framework. Whether you're automating repetitive tasks, synchronizing complex workflows, or building dashboards with external systems, this chapter equips you with the foundations to take full control of your integration environment.

Why Use Custom Scripts and APIs?

Standard tools may fall short when you need to:

- Sync data across Jira projects, Confluence spaces, or third-party apps
- Auto-generate pages or issues based on complex triggers
- Bulk-update or transition tasks based on custom rules
- Enforce workflow or documentation consistency programmatically
- Query and visualize project data externally

Custom scripts offer **precision, control, and automation** tailored to your unique use case.

Understanding the Atlassian REST API

Both Jira and Confluence provide robust **REST APIs** that let you interact with their platforms programmatically.

Jira REST API Overview

Base URL example (Cloud): `https://your-domain.atlassian.net/rest/api/3/`

Key operations include:

- Create, update, transition issues
- Fetch filters, boards, sprints
- Manage users, roles, and permissions
- Run JQL queries programmatically

Confluence REST API Overview

Base URL example (Cloud): `https://your-domain.atlassian.net/wiki/rest/api/`

Common tasks:

- Create or update pages
- Add comments, labels, or attachments
- Fetch content history
- Manage spaces and templates

Authentication usually requires an **API token** with basic auth or OAuth, especially in Atlassian Cloud environments.

Scripting Languages and Tools

You can use any HTTP-enabled scripting language (Python, JavaScript, Shell, etc.) to work with the APIs. Popular choices include:

- **Python** (requests library)
- **Node.js** (axios or node-fetch)
- **Bash + curl** (for simple automations)
- **PowerShell** (for Windows environments)
- **Java** (for enterprise-level scripts or plugins)

Sample Use Cases and Script Snippets

1. Auto-Create a Confluence Page When a New Epic Is Created in Jira

Workflow: Triggered when a Jira epic is created → Calls Confluence API → Generates a new spec page linked to the epic

Python Sample:

```python
import requests
from requests.auth import HTTPBasicAuth

auth = HTTPBasicAuth("email@example.com", "your_api_token")

headers = {
    "Accept": "application/json",
    "Content-Type": "application/json"
}

data = {
    "type": "page",
    "title": "Spec for New Epic: ABC-123",
    "space": {"key": "DEV"},
    "body": {
        "storage": {
            "value": "<p>Linked Epic: ABC-123</p>",
            "representation": "storage"
        }
    }
}
```

```
response = requests.post(
    "https://your-domain.atlassian.net/wiki/rest/api/content",
    json=data,
    headers=headers,
    auth=auth
)
```

---

2. Bulk Transition Jira Issues Based on Status and Label

Goal: Move all "In QA" issues labeled `hotfix` to "Ready for Release"

Shell Script:

```
curl -u email@example.com:API_TOKEN \
 -X POST \
 --data '{"transition":{"id":"31"}}' \
 -H "Content-Type: application/json" \
 https://your-domain.atlassian.net/rest/api/3/issue/ISSUE-KEY/transitions
```

Loop this through a JQL search to automate transitions.

---

3. Generate a Weekly Confluence Status Report from Jira Data

Flow:

- Use JQL to fetch issues updated in the past 7 days
- Format as HTML or Markdown
- Use Confluence API to create/update a report page

This allows you to replace manual reports with **automated, audit-ready summaries**.

Enhancing Automation with Marketplace Tools

You can also run custom scripts inside Jira or Confluence using scripting add-ons such as:

- **ScriptRunner for Jira/Confluence**
  - Execute Groovy scripts inside workflows or custom UI
  - Extend Jira automation rules with conditional logic
- **Automation for Jira** (built-in in Cloud)
  - Allows some scripting logic and triggers without full code
- **Adaptavist Script Libraries**
  - Offers pre-written scripts for bulk operations and integrations

These tools are ideal for non-developers or admins who want advanced logic without full API implementation.

Best Practices for Custom Integration

- **Use separate API tokens** for automation bots
- **Log all automated actions** for traceability
- **Limit permissions** of API tokens to required scopes only
- **Test in staging environments** before deploying in production
- **Document your custom scripts** for team visibility and continuity
- **Use rate limits and retries** to handle API throttling gracefully

---

Security Considerations

- Avoid hardcoding sensitive credentials in scripts—use environment variables or secret managers
- Use HTTPS exclusively for all API communication
- Regularly rotate API tokens and audit usage logs
- Consider OAuth for advanced apps that require user-level access

---

Summary

Custom scripts and APIs unlock a new level of efficiency and control over your Jira-Confluence integration. Whether you're auto-generating documentation, syncing issue states, or building custom dashboards, scripting empowers you to **scale operations, eliminate manual work, and align your tools to your exact workflows**.

Advanced Jira Filters in Confluence

Tailoring Data Views for Smarter Collaboration

For teams leveraging Jira and Confluence together, Jira filters are more than just search tools—they're the engine behind **dynamic, relevant, and real-time reporting** within Confluence. While basic filters offer quick visibility into tasks or projects, advanced filters enable you to build **custom dashboards**, **track nuanced progress**, and **generate highly specific views** tailored to your team's needs.

This chapter explores how to create, manage, and embed **advanced Jira filters inside Confluence**, transforming ordinary project pages into powerful, data-driven knowledge hubs.

Why Use Advanced Filters?

Advanced Jira filters give you more control over what data you present in Confluence. You can:

- **Target specific workstreams** (e.g., only backend bugs in QA)
- **Filter by custom fields** (e.g., team owner, component, priority)
- **Track sprint progress across multiple teams or projects**
- **Highlight exceptions** (e.g., overdue tasks or unassigned tickets)
- **Build role-specific dashboards** for PMs, developers, or executives

Combined with Confluence macros, these filters enable real-time, contextual visibility directly within project documentation.

The Foundation: JQL (Jira Query Language)

At the core of every advanced filter is JQL—Jira Query Language. It lets you perform detailed searches using logical operators, conditions, and functions.

Example Queries:

- **Unassigned Bugs by Priority** `project = PROJ AND issuetype = Bug AND assignee IS EMPTY ORDER BY priority DESC`
- **Stories Not Updated in 7 Days** `project = PROJ AND issuetype = Story AND updated <= -7d AND status != Done`
- **Open Issues Across Multiple Sprints** `project = PROJ AND sprint in openSprints() AND status in ("To Do", "In Progress")`
- **High Priority Issues for a Specific Component** `priority = High AND component = "Payment Gateway" AND status != Closed`
- **Bugs Blocked by Other Issues** `issuefunction in hasLinks("is blocked by") AND issuetype = Bug`

Tip: Use Jira's Advanced Search to build and test your filters before embedding them.

Step-by-Step: Embedding Advanced Filters in Confluence

1. Save Your Filter in Jira

1. Go to **Filters > Advanced Issue Search**
2. Write or paste your JQL query
3. Click **Save As** and name your filter clearly (e.g., "Unassigned QA Bugs – Sprint 42")

2. Insert the Filter into Confluence

On any Confluence page:

1. Click **Insert > Jira Issue/Filter**
2. Search and select your saved filter
3. Choose display options:
   - Table view
   - List view
   - Total count
4. Customize columns to show fields like Assignee, Status, or Sprint

This embeds a **live view** of filtered Jira issues, updating in real time.

Enhancing Filters with Confluence Macros

Confluence offers multiple macros to present filtered Jira data more effectively:

Macro	Description
Jira Issues Macro	Embed filtered issue tables
Jira Chart Macro	Visualize with pie, bar, or line charts
Jira Roadmap Macro	Show timeline views (Premium only)
Expand Macro	Hide complex filters or reports behind collapsible sections
Page Properties Report	Summarize filter outputs across pages (e.g., status reports)

Use Cases for Advanced Filters in Confluence

1. Sprint Dashboard for QA Team

```
project = SHOP AND sprint in openSprints() AND issuetype = Bug AND status in
("To Do", "In QA")
```

- Embedded in a Confluence page titled *"QA Sprint View – Sprint 14"*
- View is grouped by priority or assigned tester

2. Project Health Overview

```
project = WEB AND statusCategory != Done AND updated <= -3d
```

- Highlights stalled tickets
- Embedded in the *"Weekly PM Check-in"* page with a Jira Chart Macro

3. Cross-Project Epic Tracker

```
issuetype = Epic AND status != Done AND project in (APP, WEB, API)
```

- Linked from a stakeholder-facing roadmap page
- Each epic includes links to detailed Confluence requirement pages

---

Tips for Managing and Scaling Filters

- **Use naming conventions** for filters (e.g., `TeamName - Filter Purpose - Sprint #`)
- **Control filter permissions** to ensure visibility and security
- **Document filter logic** in the Confluence page for transparency
- **Use labels on pages** to organize by team, sprint, or feature
- **Group filters logically**: by project, component, or user role

---

Going Further: Dynamic Filters with Parameters

While Confluence doesn't natively support interactive filter inputs, you can simulate dynamic behavior by:

- Creating multiple tabs or expand sections for different filters
- Duplicating a page template with pre-configured filter macros
- Using apps like **Elements Connect** or **Table Filter and Charts for Confluence** to add dropdown filters, pivot tables, and visual reports

---

Summary

Advanced Jira filters embedded in Confluence allow you to transform static project pages into **live, interactive status dashboards**. Whether you're reporting to stakeholders or managing your team's backlog, using custom filters ensures that **everyone sees the most relevant, up-to-date information—right where they need it.**

Leveraging Marketplace Apps for Enhanced Functionality

Supercharge Your Jira-Confluence Integration with Purpose-Built Add-Ons

While the native integration between Jira and Confluence offers a robust foundation, many teams reach a point where **out-of-the-box features fall short** of their evolving needs. Whether it's advanced reporting, interactive data views, real-time charts, or automation workflows, the Atlassian Marketplace offers a vast ecosystem of apps designed to **extend and enhance** your collaborative framework.

This chapter explores how to identify, select, and implement the right marketplace apps to elevate your Jira-Confluence integration—and tailor it to your team's unique processes and challenges.

Why Use Marketplace Apps?

Marketplace apps offer advanced capabilities that:

- Fill functional gaps (e.g., pivot tables, Gantt charts, risk matrices)
- Automate repetitive actions beyond native automation
- Enhance UI/UX for non-technical users
- Enable better visualizations and decision-making
- Support regulatory, compliance, or governance needs

By leveraging trusted apps, you can **customize your ecosystem without building everything from scratch.**

Categories of Popular Marketplace Apps

1. Reporting and Visualization Tools

App	Use Case
eazyBI Reports and Charts	Create custom charts, pivot tables, and dashboards with advanced data analysis
Custom Charts for Jira/Confluence	Drag-and-drop chart creation with simplified UI
Rich Filters for Jira Dashboards	Build dynamic dashboards with clickable filters
Table Filter and Charts for Confluence	Add Excel-like interactivity to tables embedded in Confluence pages

2. Workflow Automation and Scripting

App	Use Case
ScriptRunner for Jira/Confluence	Automate workflows, extend JQL, run scripts, and trigger logic-based events
Automation for Jira (built-in for Cloud)	Automate transitions, comments, notifications, and more

JMWE (Jira Misc Workflow Extensions)	Add conditions, validators, and post-functions to workflows without code

3. Documentation and Collaboration Enhancers

App	Use Case
Comala Document Management	Implement review and approval workflows in Confluence
Gliffy or Draw.io Diagrams	Create wireframes, architecture diagrams, and flowcharts directly in pages
Scroll Documents	Manage Confluence pages as versioned, structured documentation sets

4. Project Management and Planning

App	Use Case
Advanced Roadmaps for Jira	High-level project planning, team capacity management (included in Jira Premium)
BigPicture / Structure	Create cross-project Gantt charts, dependencies, and resource allocations
Easy Agile User Story Maps	Visualize backlog items across epics and sprints for better planning sessions

How to Select the Right Marketplace App

1. **Define Your Use Case** Start with a clear problem or opportunity (e.g., "We need better sprint-level visual reports in Confluence").
2. **Check Compatibility** Ensure the app works with your Jira/Confluence version (Cloud, Server, or Data Center).
3. **Evaluate Security & Reviews**
   - Look for apps with high ratings and active support
   - For sensitive data, verify if the app is **Cloud Fortified** or has SOC2 compliance
4. **Trial and Experiment** Most apps offer a 30-day free trial. Set up a test project to validate whether it fits your workflow.
5. **Monitor Performance Impact** For Server/Data Center instances, make sure the app doesn't affect load times or system stability.

Example Use Case: Combining ScriptRunner + Confluence Charts

Challenge: Your team wants to automatically generate a weekly sprint summary page in Confluence that includes Jira issue breakdowns, blockers, and resolved bugs.

Solution:

- Use **ScriptRunner for Jira** to schedule a script that compiles the required issues every Friday
- The script then triggers a Confluence API call that populates a page template
- Use **Jira Chart Macro** and **Table Filter and Charts** to present the data cleanly

The result? A **fully automated sprint report** with minimal manual input and always up to date.

Governance Tip: Managing Apps at Scale

As your Atlassian environment grows:

- Maintain a **registry of approved apps** with owner and use case documentation
- Periodically **review app usage** and remove redundant or underused apps
- For large teams, create an **App Request Process** to evaluate new app proposals

---

Cost Considerations

- Most apps charge **per user, per month**, and the pricing varies across Cloud vs. Data Center deployments
- Bundle apps smartly—some vendors offer discounts if you use multiple apps from the same suite
- Factor in **ROI from time saved, risk mitigated, or reporting improved**

Summary

Marketplace apps empower teams to go beyond default capabilities and **tailor Jira-Confluence workflows to specific goals, industries, and team dynamics**. With thousands of apps available, the key lies in choosing wisely—balancing feature power, usability, and governance. When used correctly, these tools don't just enhance your platform—they transform it into a **custom-fit digital workspace.**

Customizing Workflows for Cross-Platform Efficiency

Bridging the Gaps Between Tools, Teams, and Tasks

When teams rely on both Jira and Confluence, the ultimate goal is to create a **unified workflow** that flows naturally across platforms. While Jira excels at task tracking and structured process enforcement, Confluence brings flexibility and context to planning, documentation, and collaboration. By customizing workflows across these tools, you enable your teams to **move faster, reduce friction, and stay aligned without duplication or confusion.**

This chapter explores how to design and implement **cross-platform workflows** that feel seamless, are easy to adopt, and boost operational efficiency—especially for teams working across functions, locations, or disciplines.

What Is a Cross-Platform Workflow?

A cross-platform workflow integrates **structured actions in Jira** with **contextual collaboration in Confluence**—automating the flow of information, updates, approvals, and documentation across both.

For example:

- A product manager creates a **feature spec in Confluence**, which links to a corresponding Jira epic.
- Developers break that epic into **Jira stories**, while linking to the Confluence spec.
- QA logs bugs in Jira that auto-tag related documentation in Confluence.
- Status reports are **automatically generated** in Confluence using Jira macros.

Why Customize Workflows?

Out-of-the-box workflows may be too rigid or generic for real-world needs. Custom workflows allow you to:

- Align tools with **team-specific processes**
- Reduce manual steps and eliminate double work
- Add automation triggers across platforms
- Create **documentation-to-execution pipelines**
- Enforce governance while preserving flexibility

When tailored effectively, custom workflows turn Jira and Confluence into **one fluid experience.**

Common Cross-Platform Workflow Patterns

1. Requirements to Delivery

Confluence → Jira

- Create a product requirements document (PRD) in Confluence
- Use Smart Links or the Jira Issues Macro to **embed epics and stories**
- Link Jira epics back to the PRD from within Jira

- As development progresses, **status updates automatically reflect** on the Confluence page

Tip: Use templates in Confluence for repeatable requirement structures, with pre-configured Jira macros.

2. Content Review and Approval Workflow

Confluence ↔ Jira

- Authoring team drafts documentation in Confluence
- Create a Jira issue for review task and link to the Confluence page
- Add an approval checklist and transition statuses in Jira (e.g., "Draft," "In Review," "Approved")
- Confluence status macros reflect the Jira issue state dynamically

This is ideal for technical writers, legal reviewers, or regulated industries.

3. Sprint Planning and Execution

Jira → Confluence

- Planning done in a Confluence page using sprint templates
- Sprint backlog pulled from Jira with JQL macros
- Page includes embedded velocity charts, team assignments, and risk flags
- Issues resolved in Jira automatically update the sprint dashboard

Use this to run sprint planning sessions with everything in one place.

Custom Workflow Enhancements

1. Add Jira Triggers to Notify or Update Confluence Pages

Using **Automation for Jira**, you can:

- Post a comment to a Confluence page when a Jira ticket changes status
- Send an email/slack with a Confluence page link when a task is created or resolved
- Update Confluence labels or task lists via REST API calls triggered from Jira

2. Use Confluence Blueprints with Jira Integration

Create custom **Confluence blueprints** that prompt users to enter key project details, and:

- Automatically generate linked Jira issues
- Insert Jira filter macros with predefined logic
- Apply page labels to trigger workflows or organize dashboards

3. Automate Jira Transitions Based on Confluence Activity

If you're using **ScriptRunner** or Jira REST API integrations, you can:

- Transition Jira issues when a linked Confluence page is edited or approved
- Enforce that documentation must be linked before issue transitions to "Ready for QA"
- Close documentation tasks when a page is published or moved to a final space

This approach is ideal for compliance-focused teams needing traceability.

Design Considerations for Effective Workflow Customization

- **Start with a clear map**: Identify roles, tasks, and tool responsibilities
- **Minimize context switching**: Use macros and linking to unify content
- **Balance structure and flexibility**: Allow freeform notes but standardize key checkpoints
- **Test with real users**: Pilot the workflow before full rollout
- **Document your workflow**: Create a visual flowchart or checklist in Confluence for onboarding

---

Example: Workflow for Bug-to-Knowledge Base Pipeline

1. **Bug reported in Jira** → status = "Confirmed"
2. Linked Confluence page auto-created with troubleshooting steps
3. Developer updates both Jira ticket and Confluence doc during fix
4. Upon resolution, a Confluence label is added: `kb-ready`
5. A reviewer publishes the doc into the public-facing knowledge base space

This ensures **every resolved bug results in searchable, accessible knowledge**.

Summary

Customizing workflows across Jira and Confluence enables your teams to **eliminate silos**, improve traceability, and streamline collaboration. By designing with clarity, automation, and role alignment in mind, you can turn these tools into a synchronized system that **adapts to your organization—not the other way around.**

Section 7:
Troubleshooting and Optimization

Common Integration Pitfalls and Fixes

Navigating the Most Frequent Challenges in Jira-Confluence Integration

Even the most well-planned Jira-Confluence integration can run into roadblocks. From configuration oversights to permission mismatches and data silos, these pitfalls can undermine your collaboration goals and slow down your team's productivity. The good news? Most integration issues are well-documented, predictable, and solvable.

In this chapter, we'll highlight the most common integration problems that teams face—and offer practical solutions and preventative measures to ensure your Jira-Confluence ecosystem runs smoothly and reliably.

Pitfall 1: Broken or Missing Links Between Jira and Confluence

Symptoms:

- Jira issues fail to appear in Confluence macros
- Confluence pages don't reflect linked Jira data
- "Unknown Jira link" or "Unable to load content" errors

Root Causes:

- Jira and Confluence are not properly connected via **Application Links**
- User lacks access to both tools
- Macros are referencing deleted or renamed filters/issues/pages

Fixes:

- Go to **Jira Administration > Application Links**, ensure proper bidirectional linking with Confluence
- Check user permissions for both Jira and Confluence
- Validate JQL filters used in Confluence pages
- Replace or remove invalid macros or Smart Links

Prevention Tip: Test new page templates or macros in a staging space before applying globally.

Pitfall 2: Permission Conflicts Across Platforms

Symptoms:

- Jira issues appear blank when embedded in Confluence
- Users see "You don't have access" messages for linked items
- Workflow triggers or automation rules silently fail

Root Causes:

- Permissions are granted in one platform but not the other
- Anonymous or restricted Confluence pages linking to restricted Jira projects
- Users working across multiple projects with inconsistent role definitions

Fixes:

- Align permission groups across Jira and Confluence (e.g., use centralized user directories or synchronized groups)
- Avoid using anonymous access where possible
- Review permission schemes in Jira and space/page restrictions in Confluence

Prevention Tip: Document a permission matrix outlining who can see, edit, or comment on shared artifacts.

Pitfall 3: Inconsistent Naming and Linking Conventions

Symptoms:

- Difficulty finding linked content
- Duplicate issues or Confluence pages
- Confusion about the "source of truth"

Root Causes:

- Ad hoc creation of links and pages
- Inconsistent page titles or issue summaries
- Manual linking instead of Smart Links or macros

Fixes:

- Establish and enforce naming conventions for pages (e.g., [Project]-[Feature]-Spec) and Jira issues
- Train teams to use Smart Links and Jira Macros instead of plain URLs
- Periodically audit and clean up outdated or duplicate links

Prevention Tip: Use Confluence templates and Jira issue templates with built-in link placeholders.

Pitfall 4: Automation Failures or Unintended Triggers

Symptoms:

- Automated updates don't execute
- Pages or issues update at the wrong time
- Excessive or missing notifications

Root Causes:

- Broken API tokens or expired credentials
- Poorly defined rules in **Automation for Jira** or **ScriptRunner**
- Circular triggers creating loops or conflicts

Fixes:

- Review automation logs in Jira and Confluence
- Simplify automation rules and clearly separate manual vs. triggered steps
- Regenerate API tokens periodically and store them securely

Prevention Tip: Use sandbox environments to test new automation before deploying to production.

Pitfall 5: Performance Degradation Due to Heavy Macros

Symptoms:

- Confluence pages load slowly or time out
- Jira dashboards are unresponsive
- Browsers struggle to render large data sets

Root Causes:

- Overuse of Jira Macros displaying hundreds of issues
- Pages embedding multiple dynamic charts and filters
- Excessive nesting of macros within macros

Fixes:

- Use filters to limit issues to a manageable number (e.g., `maxResults = 50`)
- Paginate large views or link out to filtered views in Jira
- Replace macros with static summaries or snapshots when appropriate

Prevention Tip: Use Jira Chart Macros sparingly and always validate load times on slower connections.

Pitfall 6: Outdated Integration Plugins or Platform Mismatch

Symptoms:

- Features suddenly stop working after an update
- Macros or app links show compatibility errors
- Jira/Confluence API calls return authentication errors

Root Causes:

- Using legacy plugins incompatible with the latest Jira or Confluence version
- Self-hosted instances missing security patches or upgrades
- Deprecated REST endpoints or app features

Fixes:

- Regularly update plugins, add-ons, and Atlassian platforms
- Monitor vendor changelogs and Atlassian deprecation notices
- Use versioned API calls and error handling in custom scripts

Prevention Tip: Schedule quarterly maintenance windows to test upgrades and ensure app compatibility.

Pitfall 7: Lack of Integration Governance

Symptoms:

- Confusion over processes
- Inconsistent documentation and tool usage
- "Shadow integrations" created outside IT oversight

Root Causes:

- No standardized onboarding, templates, or usage guidelines
- Multiple teams managing integrations independently
- Poor communication between Confluence and Jira admins

Fixes:

- Create an **Integration Governance Guide**: Who owns what, tool usage best practices, escalation procedures
- Centralize automation management under an admin or DevOps lead
- Use Confluence to host documentation, process flows, and SOPs

Prevention Tip: Appoint a Jira-Confluence integration owner or committee in your organization.

Summary

Integration issues can stall productivity and undermine trust in your systems—but they're also preventable. By understanding the most common pitfalls and addressing them proactively with **permissions hygiene, process discipline, and performance best practices**, your Jira-Confluence setup can remain a dependable and powerful collaboration engine.

Ensuring Data Consistency Across Platforms

Keeping Jira and Confluence in Sync for Reliable Collaboration

Data consistency is critical to maintaining trust, efficiency, and accuracy across any integrated toolset—and Jira and Confluence are no exception. As teams scale and the flow of information multiplies, **mismatched statuses, outdated pages, and unsynced records** can derail projects, delay decisions, and create silos. To achieve true seamless collaboration, your integrated system must ensure that **changes in one platform are reflected clearly and correctly in the other**.

This chapter outlines the challenges of maintaining cross-platform consistency and provides proven strategies, tools, and habits to ensure that your Jira and Confluence environments stay **accurate, aligned, and audit-ready**.

Why Data Consistency Matters

In an integrated Jira-Confluence setup, data inconsistencies can lead to:

- **Misinformed decisions** based on outdated or conflicting information
- **Redundant work** from disconnected teams updating content in isolation
- **Reduced confidence** in reports, dashboards, or documentation
- **Compliance risks** where audit trails and traceability are required

Consistency ensures that **what you see in Confluence reflects the actual state in Jira**, and vice versa—creating a single, trustworthy source of truth.

Common Causes of Inconsistencies

1. **Manual Copy-Paste Between Systems**
   - Static content in Confluence becomes outdated as Jira issues evolve.
2. **Improper Use of Macros or Filters**
   - Macros showing incomplete data due to broken JQL filters or outdated saved searches.
3. **Lack of Bi-directional Linking**
   - Jira issues not linking to related Confluence pages and vice versa.
4. **Siloed Permission Models**
   - Users with access to one tool but not the other create misaligned updates.
5. **Overuse of Static Text Instead of Dynamic Embeds**
   - Teams summarize Jira tasks in paragraphs rather than using live issue tables.

Strategies for Maintaining Data Consistency

1. Use Jira Macros for Real-Time Data

Avoid manually listing tasks or statuses in Confluence. Instead:

- Use the **Jira Issues Macro** to embed real-time issue tables
- Filter by sprint, label, or assignee using JQL
- Display fields like Status, Assignee, and Due Date for live status checks

Bonus Tip: Set "Maximum Issues" in the macro settings to prevent slow load times on large lists.

---

2. Leverage Smart Links for Page-Issue Connections

Whenever referencing Jira issues in Confluence:

- Use **Smart Links** (paste the Jira issue URL and select "Display as Inline" or "Card")
- This ensures auto-updating titles, statuses, and direct navigation

Similarly, in Jira:

- Link to Confluence pages in the **Issue Description or Comments** section
- Create automated triggers to require a linked page for epics or stories

---

3. Automate Cross-Platform Updates

Using **Automation for Jira** or apps like **ScriptRunner**, you can:

- Automatically comment on a Confluence page when a linked Jira issue is resolved
- Notify stakeholders in Jira when a Confluence page is edited
- Transition Jira issues when related documentation reaches a defined approval state

---

4. Establish and Enforce Templates

Create **Confluence templates** with built-in Jira macros, Smart Links, and checklists. For example:

- Requirements template that includes a section for linking Jira Epics
- Sprint Review template that auto-pulls tasks completed in the current sprint
- Knowledge base article template with a "Related Jira Issue" macro block

This reduces variation and helps enforce a consistent documentation style.

---

5. Schedule Regular Reviews and Cleanup

Data consistency isn't a one-time task. Build maintenance into your workflow:

- **Monthly audits** of orphaned Jira issues or Confluence pages
- Use **saved filters** in Jira to find unresolved issues with missing links
- Run **Confluence content reports** to find outdated or unmodified pages

---

Integrating with BI and Reporting Tools

For large teams or enterprise environments:

- Use apps like **eazyBI**, **Custom Charts**, or **Table Filter and Charts** to aggregate Jira and Confluence data
- Integrate Jira data into **Confluence dashboards** for project-wide reporting
- Export filtered issue lists to Confluence tables for versioned documentation

These ensure that reports are pulling **from live, consistent sources** and reduce manual updates.

Governance Tips for Sustained Consistency

- **Assign integration ownership** to a Jira-Confluence admin or workflow coordinator
- **Train teams** on how and when to use dynamic vs. static content
- **Audit permission schemes** to ensure visibility doesn't lead to fragmentation
- **Label pages and issues consistently** to support filtered macros and automation
- Maintain a **cross-platform glossary** in Confluence to align terminology and naming conventions

---

Summary

Inconsistent data leads to inconsistent outcomes. By embracing dynamic linking, automation, standardized templates, and regular health checks, you can create a Jira-Confluence system that stays accurate and up-to-date—even as projects grow in complexity. **Consistency fuels trust, and trust fuels momentum.**

Performance Optimization for Large Teams

Keeping Your Jira-Confluence Integration Fast, Reliable, and Scalable

As your team grows, so does the complexity of your Jira and Confluence environments. With hundreds or thousands of users, projects, and pages in play, even a well-integrated system can suffer from **slow load times, system lag, or data bottlenecks** if performance optimization is overlooked. This chapter focuses on strategies to ensure your integrated Jira-Confluence setup remains fast, scalable, and user-friendly—even under enterprise-level demand.

Why Performance Declines at Scale

Larger teams and growing data volumes put pressure on several system layers:

- **User interface lag** from overloaded dashboards or large Confluence pages
- **Search delays** due to extensive issue/page indexing
- **Slow macros** embedded with too many Jira issues
- **API throttling or timeouts** when multiple automations run concurrently
- **Workflow complexity** that creates inefficient transitions and data processing

For sustained speed and reliability, optimization must be **proactive, ongoing, and holistic**.

Key Areas of Optimization

1. Optimize Jira Issue Filters and Macros in Confluence

Problem: Confluence pages slow down when displaying too many issues through Jira macros.

Solutions:

- Use **specific JQL filters** (avoid `project = XYZ` without limits)
- Limit results with `maxResults`, pagination, or a narrow time frame
- Display only necessary columns (avoid loading heavy custom fields)
- Use summary charts or counts instead of full tables for executive views

Tip: Use multiple, focused macros instead of one massive issue table.

---

2. Streamline Dashboards and Pages

Problem: Jira dashboards and Confluence homepages that pull too much real-time data slow down dramatically.

Solutions:

- Prioritize **per-team dashboards** over global ones
- Replace real-time charts with **weekly snapshots** where possible
- Archive or delete old dashboards no longer in use
- Minimize macro nesting in Confluence (e.g., avoid Jira macros inside expand macros inside tables)

---

3. Review and Simplify Workflows

Problem: Overengineered workflows can slow issue transitions and create technical debt.

Solutions:

- Audit Jira workflows regularly to remove redundant statuses or transitions
- Reduce the number of **validators, post functions, and conditions** that trigger on each transition
- Consolidate similar workflows across projects using **shared schemes**

Tip: Use workflow schemes to standardize processes and improve maintenance efficiency.

---

4. Scale User Management and Permissions

Problem: Permission checks slow down queries and page rendering when too many nested group rules exist.

Solutions:

- Use **flat, consistent permission groups**
- Minimize page-level restrictions in Confluence when space-level permissions suffice
- Deactivate inactive users or projects to reduce processing load

Tip: Set clear policies on who can create Confluence spaces or Jira projects to prevent sprawl.

---

5. Monitor Automation and API Usage

Problem: Competing automations or custom scripts create race conditions, timeouts, or update conflicts.

Solutions:

- Audit automation rules to identify unnecessary or overlapping triggers
- Use **scheduled automations** during low-traffic hours
- Monitor **API rate limits** and usage quotas, especially for integrations with third-party apps

---

6. Implement Archiving and Content Lifecycle Management

Problem: Confluence pages and Jira issues pile up over time, reducing search and navigation efficiency.

Solutions:

- Archive completed Jira projects quarterly
- Move outdated Confluence pages to an archive space or label them with `archive-*`
- Use apps like **Better Content Archiving** to automate cleanup suggestions

---

Tools for Performance Monitoring

- **Atlassian Admin Insights** – View usage trends, active users, and project stats
- **Audit Logs** – Track system changes that may introduce performance lags

- **Third-party analytics tools** like eazyBI or Arsenale Dataplane – Analyze query response time and content usage
- **Application Monitoring Platforms** (e.g., Datadog, New Relic) – For self-managed Data Center deployments

---

Collaboration Tips for Large Teams

- Create **team-specific spaces** in Confluence and projects in Jira to localize load
- Establish **governance roles** (e.g., content manager, Jira admin, automation lead)
- Train users to **use filters and links** effectively rather than building large, static pages
- Encourage the use of **watchers**, mentions, and comments instead of duplicating content for visibility

---

Summary

Performance optimization isn't just about speed—it's about ensuring **scalability, usability, and sustainability**. By tuning filters, workflows, content volume, and automation logic, large teams can continue to collaborate seamlessly without sacrificing system responsiveness. Proactive optimization gives your growing team the confidence to rely on Jira and Confluence as their go-to project ecosystem.

Security Best Practices for Shared Environments

Safeguarding Your Jira-Confluence Integration in Collaborative Workspaces

As teams scale and more users interact across Jira and Confluence, the risk surface expands—making **security and access control a non-negotiable priority**. Whether you're managing internal teams, external collaborators, or compliance-driven workflows, protecting sensitive project data requires deliberate strategy and structure.

This chapter focuses on **best practices to secure shared Jira-Confluence environments**, ensuring your integration supports collaboration without compromising confidentiality, integrity, or availability.

Understanding the Shared Environment Risk Landscape

In shared environments—especially across departments, vendors, or remote teams—common security risks include:

- **Unauthorized access** to confidential issues or pages
- **Accidental data leaks** via misconfigured permissions
- **Excessive user rights** leading to uncontrolled changes
- **Integration abuse** through API misuse or weak authentication
- **Lack of audit visibility** on who did what and when

A secure integration protects against both **external threats and internal mishandling**.

---

1. Establish Role-Based Access Controls (RBAC)

Why it matters: Broad permissions increase exposure. RBAC ensures users only see and do what they need to.

Best Practices:

- Define roles (e.g., Contributor, Viewer, Admin) across both platforms
- Use **groups**, not individuals, for permission assignment
- Align roles across Jira and Confluence to ensure parity
- Limit admin access to a small, trusted group

Tip: Review user group memberships quarterly to catch drift or outdated roles.

---

2. Secure Spaces and Projects with Layered Permissions

Why it matters: Project and space permissions are your first line of defense.

Best Practices:

- Use **space-level restrictions** in Confluence for sensitive content (e.g., HR, finance, legal)
- In Jira, set up **project permission schemes** based on team structure
- Avoid using anonymous or public access unless absolutely necessary
- Apply **page-level restrictions** only when needed (too many can lead to confusion)

---

3. Apply Principle of Least Privilege

Why it matters: The fewer privileges a user has, the less potential damage from error or misuse.

Best Practices:

- Start all users at the lowest necessary role
- Avoid granting global access unless justified (e.g., system admin, audit team)
- Don't give editing rights if viewing is sufficient (especially in Confluence)
- Use **read-only roles** for third-party vendors or stakeholders

---

4. Enforce Strong Authentication and Identity Management

Why it matters: Credentials are a common attack vector.

Best Practices:

- Enforce **single sign-on (SSO)** and **multi-factor authentication (MFA)**
- Integrate with identity providers like Okta, Azure AD, or Google Workspace
- Use **SCIM** for automated user provisioning and deprovisioning
- Immediately revoke access when an employee or contractor exits

*Bonus Tip: Enable **session timeouts** and idle user logouts for added protection.*

---

5. Secure Integration Points and API Access

Why it matters: APIs and third-party plugins can introduce vulnerabilities.

Best Practices:

- Audit and approve all installed apps and plugins (Jira/Confluence Marketplace)
- Rotate API tokens regularly and monitor their usage
- Use OAuth 2.0 for secure app authentication
- Log and monitor outbound requests from integrations

Tip: Keep an inventory of all integrations and their scope of access.

---

6. Monitor Activity with Audit Logs and Alerts

Why it matters: Visibility allows you to detect and respond to suspicious behavior.

Best Practices:

- Enable **audit logging** in both Jira and Confluence (available in Premium/Data Center plans)
- Monitor for events like permission changes, bulk edits, and failed login attempts
- Set up alerts for high-risk changes, such as new admin additions
- Review logs weekly or integrate with SIEM tools (e.g., Splunk, Datadog)

---

7. Train Users on Security-Aware Collaboration

Why it matters: Even strong systems fail under poor user behavior.

Best Practices:

- Educate teams on **safe sharing** (e.g., never posting private Jira links in public Confluence spaces)
- Promote awareness of **phishing or social engineering**
- Create a **security usage guide** specific to your Jira-Confluence environment
- Encourage reporting of suspicious activity

Bonus Tip: Include "security checklists" in project kickoffs to reinforce responsible use.

---

8. Maintain a Security Incident Response Plan

Why it matters: If something goes wrong, speed and structure are key.

Best Practices:

- Define escalation paths for security incidents (e.g., data exposure, credential theft)
- Have backup and recovery plans for both Jira and Confluence
- Regularly back up spaces, projects, and database snapshots
- Conduct drills to test your response readiness

Summary

Security in a shared Jira-Confluence environment is not a one-time setup—it's an ongoing practice of vigilance, governance, and accountability. By enforcing layered access controls, managing identities tightly, monitoring activity, and educating users, you can create an integration that **empowers collaboration without compromising trust**.

Section 8:
Real-World Use Cases

Case Study: Agile Software Development Teams

How Agile Teams Achieve Seamless Collaboration with Jira and Confluence

Agile software development thrives on clarity, responsiveness, and collaboration. From sprint planning to backlog grooming, the need for synchronized documentation and task tracking is continuous—and often chaotic without the right tooling. In this case study, we explore how a mid-sized software company used **Jira and Confluence integration** to streamline their development process, improve team visibility, and accelerate delivery cycles.

Company Profile

- **Company**: DevSync Technologies
- **Size**: 80-person engineering team
- **Industry**: SaaS (Software-as-a-Service)
- **Teams Using Integration**: Product Managers, Developers, QA, DevOps, UX/UI
- **Challenge**: Disconnected workflows between product specs (Confluence) and sprint execution (Jira)

The Problem

Before integration:

- **Product requirements** were scattered across emails, Confluence pages, and PDFs
- **Developers** frequently worked on Jira tickets without full context
- **QA teams** lacked access to the original acceptance criteria or wireframes
- **Standups and retrospectives** relied on manually prepared slides or spreadsheets
- **New team members** struggled to understand feature histories or sprint goals

The lack of a unified source of truth led to:

- Misaligned expectations
- Duplicate work
- Delays in sprint execution
- Frequent rework due to missed details

The Solution: Jira-Confluence Integration Strategy

1. Sprint Documentation Hub in Confluence

Each sprint had its own Confluence page that included:

- Goals and themes for the sprint
- Linked Jira boards filtered by the current sprint
- Smart links to epics and user stories
- Embedded product requirements using Jira Issue Macros
- A sprint calendar with key events and demos

Outcome: Team members could quickly orient themselves to the sprint scope and access all related tickets and documentation from one page.

---

2. Product Requirement Templates with Embedded Jira Epics

The Product team standardized feature specs using a Confluence template that included:

- Problem statement and feature overview
- Acceptance criteria
- Personas and user stories
- Design mockups from Figma
- Linked Jira Epic (via Smart Link)
- Live issue tables for subtasks and related bugs

Outcome: Developers and QA always had context, and specs evolved in tandem with implementation.

---

3. Automated Workflows and Cross-Linking

Using **Automation for Jira** and page templates:

- When a new Epic was created, a corresponding Confluence page was auto-generated using a specific template
- When a Confluence page was published with a "Ready for Dev" label, the linked Jira issue was auto-transitioned to "To Do"
- Team leads received Slack alerts whenever a page linked to a high-priority bug was updated

Outcome: Time was saved, status remained accurate, and manual tracking was minimized.

---

4. Post-Sprint Retrospectives in Confluence

After each sprint:

- A retrospective page was created using a standardized template
- Team members added wins, challenges, and improvements asynchronously
- Jira charts were embedded to visualize sprint velocity, issue churn, and bug count
- Action items were created as Jira tasks and linked back to the page

Outcome: Retros became more actionable and transparent, helping foster a culture of continuous improvement.

Benefits Observed

Metric	Before Integration	After Integration
Average Sprint Completion Rate	72%	93%
Developer Time Spent in Meetings	High	Reduced by 30%
Ticket Rework Due to Misalignment	Frequent	Rare
Time to Onboard New Team Members	~2 weeks	< 1 week
Visibility Across Functions	Low	High (Single Source)

Lessons Learned

- **Integration requires training**: Early adoption was slow until teams were trained to use templates and macros effectively.
- **Keep it simple**: Not every page needs dynamic charts or embedded boards—only use what adds clarity.
- **Assign ownership**: Each Confluence space had a page steward to ensure content stayed relevant and linked.
- **Iterate on templates**: Feedback from developers and QA helped evolve spec templates into powerful alignment tools.

Summary

By tightly integrating Jira and Confluence, DevSync Technologies transformed its agile workflow from fragmented and reactive to **synchronized, efficient, and transparent**. From product ideation to post-release analysis, every step of the software development lifecycle now lives in a shared, live ecosystem—empowering teams to collaborate without friction.

Case Study: Remote Team Collaboration

Unifying Distributed Teams with a Seamless Jira-Confluence Integration

In today's increasingly remote-first world, distributed teams face a unique set of collaboration challenges. Misaligned communication, siloed information, and inconsistent workflows often stand in the way of productivity. This case study illustrates how **a fully remote product and engineering team** leveraged Jira and Confluence integration to overcome these hurdles and achieve real-time collaboration across multiple time zones.

Organization Overview

- **Company**: CloudNova Solutions
- **Team Size**: 60 remote employees across 6 countries
- **Departments Involved**: Product, Engineering, Customer Success, QA
- **Primary Challenge**: Collaboration gaps due to asynchronous work and communication silos
- **Tools Before Integration**: Slack, Trello, Google Docs, scattered Confluence use

---

The Problem

Despite using modern tools, CloudNova struggled with:

- **Unclear handoffs** between teams
- Difficulty tracking progress on features or bugs
- Multiple versions of product requirements across platforms
- Delayed feedback due to time zone differences
- No unified project view for leadership and cross-functional partners

The result: duplicate efforts, longer cycle times, and missed deadlines.

The Integration Approach

To centralize communication and streamline workflows, CloudNova adopted a **Jira-Confluence integration strategy** centered around three principles: **visibility, accessibility, and real-time linkage**.

---

1. Centralized Virtual Workspaces

How: Every project had its own Confluence space linked directly to a corresponding Jira project.

Features included:

- Project overview with objectives and key results (OKRs)
- Pages with live Jira filters for issues by assignee, status, or priority
- Project timeline embedded with [Roadmap macro]
- Dynamic reports showing open bugs, blockers, and sprint burndown charts

Result: All stakeholders, regardless of time zone, had a single destination for project context and updates.

---

2. Daily Standup Automation

How: A Confluence template was created for asynchronous daily updates. Each team member filled it out at their local time.

Template Sections:

- What I did yesterday
- What I plan to do today
- Any blockers (linked to Jira tickets)
- Feedback needed (with mentions or labels)

Bonus: Jira comments and ticket links embedded in the Confluence page for traceability.

Result: The team eliminated real-time standups, yet remained fully aligned.

---

3. Linked Knowledge Base for Customer Success

How: Customer Success team created a Confluence knowledge base auto-linked to Jira issues with labels like `known-issue`, `waiting-on-fix`, or `feature-request`.

Features:

- Real-time visibility into issue status from within the KB
- Automatic updates to Confluence pages when Jira statuses changed
- Jira Automation triggered Slack alerts to the support team when critical issues moved to "In Progress"

Result: Drastically improved support response times and reduced back-and-forth between dev and support.

---

4. Onboarding and Documentation Repository

How: Created a single onboarding portal in Confluence with:

- Role-specific task lists linked to Jira issues
- Workflow diagrams
- Integration how-tos
- Pages filtered by project/team tags

Result: Reduced onboarding time from 2 weeks to 5 days for new remote hires.

Benefits Achieved

KPI	Before Integration	After Integration
Feature Development Cycle Time	18 days	11 days
Number of Lost or Duplicated Tasks	Frequent	Rare

Support Escalation Resolution Time	48 hours avg.	< 24 hours
Internal Meeting Hours per Week	~12 hours	~5 hours
Cross-Time Zone Project Visibility	Low	High

Key Lessons and Best Practices

- **Asynchronous collaboration** requires structure—Confluence templates and Jira automation help set that structure.
- **Live linkage is essential**: Relying on manual status updates leads to confusion; embedded Jira macros and smart links eliminate that.
- **Shared dashboards** across departments align everyone, not just the product team.
- **Remote teams thrive on autonomy**—a centralized knowledge system empowers team members to get answers without waiting.

Summary

By embracing Jira and Confluence integration, CloudNova created a collaborative ecosystem that transcended physical and temporal boundaries. Their success proves that **geography doesn't have to limit alignment or productivity**—not when your tools are integrated to act as a digital workspace for every stakeholder.

Case Study: Enterprise-Level Project Governance

How a Fortune 500 Company Standardized Collaboration and Oversight with Jira-Confluence Integration

In large organizations, managing projects across multiple departments, regions, and reporting lines presents significant challenges. When various teams use disconnected tools and processes, it leads to fractured visibility, inconsistent reporting, and compliance gaps. This case study explores how a **Fortune 500 enterprise** used Jira and Confluence to implement **scalable, governance-driven project management**—all without sacrificing agility or collaboration.

Organization Overview

- **Company**: Stratacore Global
- **Employees**: 25,000+
- **Offices**: Across North America, Europe, and APAC
- **Departments Involved**: Product, IT, PMO, Compliance, Finance, Marketing
- **Problem**: Lack of unified governance for cross-departmental programs and regulatory oversight

---

The Challenge

Stratacore's project portfolio included hundreds of initiatives running simultaneously across business units. Before integration:

- **PMOs used Excel or PowerPoint** to track timelines and deliverables
- **Teams used a mix of Trello, Basecamp, and legacy ticketing systems**
- **Status reporting was manual**, inconsistent, and often delayed
- **Audit trails** for compliance-critical work were hard to generate
- **Leadership had no real-time portfolio view**

This fragmented system created operational inefficiencies, accountability issues, and exposure to regulatory risk.

The Integration Solution

The enterprise rolled out **Jira for work execution** and **Confluence for documentation and reporting**, with strict governance controls layered through configuration, templates, and automation.

---

1. Program-Level Dashboards in Confluence

Each business program had a standardized Confluence dashboard with:

- High-level goals and KPIs
- Embedded Jira Portfolio Roadmap view
- Aggregated issue statuses from multiple Jira projects
- Visual risk matrix (linked to tracked Jira issues)
- Real-time metrics: delivery progress, overdue tasks, budget status

Result: Executives could monitor portfolio health without requesting manual updates.

---

2. Governance Workflow Templates

Confluence spaces were provisioned using templates tailored for:

- **IT governance and change management**
- **Risk mitigation and audit prep**
- **Product lifecycle tracking (from ideation to deprecation)**

Each page automatically included:

- Mandatory compliance checklists
- Linked Jira issue tables filtered by governance tags (e.g., `SOX-required`, `PII-sensitive`)
- E-signature and approval macros
- Comments and decision logs for traceability

Result: Governance was built into daily workflows, not bolted on afterward.

---

3. Unified Intake and Approval Processes

All project requests, no matter the department, flowed through a **Confluence intake form** integrated with Jira's automation engine.

Workflow:

1. Stakeholder fills Confluence form
2. Jira ticket automatically created and routed to governance board
3. Reviewers are auto-notified with SLA timers
4. Status changes update both Jira and Confluence dynamically

Result: No more rogue projects; all initiatives entered a transparent, reviewable workflow.

---

4. Regulatory Compliance Tracking

Compliance teams used custom Jira workflows to track:

- GDPR data-handling approvals
- SOX and HIPAA requirements
- Vendor security assessments

Confluence housed all related documentation, including:

- Signed policies
- Audit evidence links
- History of Jira workflow transitions (with timestamps and actors)

Result: Audit readiness improved and audit fatigue decreased—no more scrambling for data trails.

Outcomes Achieved

Metric	Before Integration	After Integration
Weekly Reporting Prep Time	~8 hours per manager	~30 minutes
Audit Preparation Time (Quarterly)	~3 weeks	< 1 week
Project Approval Cycle Time	~21 days	~8 days
Duplicate Tool Use Across Teams	High	Low (Standardized)
Cross-Departmental Visibility and Alignment	Limited	Unified and Transparent

Strategic Benefits

- **PMO standardization** across regions without disrupting team autonomy
- **Live executive reporting** with drill-down capabilities
- **Reduced operational risk** through consistent documentation and controls
- **Scalable framework** that adapts to changing regulatory environments
- **Improved trust and accountability** from leadership to frontline teams

Summary

This case study demonstrates that Jira and Confluence aren't just tools for agile teams—they're robust platforms for **enterprise-grade project governance**. By unifying project execution, compliance, and reporting into an integrated ecosystem, Stratacore turned complexity into clarity—and ensured their project framework could scale with confidence.

Section 9:
Scaling and Future-Proofing

Scaling Integration for Growing Teams

Preparing Jira-Confluence Integration to Support Expansion Without Chaos

As teams grow in size and complexity, the systems that once worked effortlessly can quickly become bottlenecks. For companies using Jira and Confluence to streamline collaboration, scaling their integration is not just about adding more users—it's about **sustaining clarity, performance, and governance** as the number of projects, contributors, and workflows multiply.

This chapter outlines how to architect and evolve your Jira-Confluence integration to support growing teams—without compromising usability or efficiency.

Understanding the Impact of Team Growth

Before scaling your integration, recognize the challenges that arise when your team expands:

- **Increased project volume** across departments
- **Duplication of workflows and documentation**
- **Greater need for role-based permissions and visibility control**
- **Conflicting automation rules or overlapping integrations**
- **System performance degradation** (especially in Jira)

If left unchecked, these issues can erode the very collaboration your integration was meant to enhance.

---

1. Standardize Project Templates and Confluence Spaces

As new teams or departments onboard, inconsistency in project setup can lead to confusion.

How to scale it:

- **Use Jira project templates** with predefined issue types, workflows, boards, and permissions.
- **Create Confluence space blueprints** for different project types (Agile delivery, ITSM, product development, etc.)
- **Link templates with automation** to auto-create spaces when a new Jira project is initiated.

Benefit:

Ensures consistent structure and reduces onboarding friction for new teams.

---

2. Implement Role-Based Permission Schemes

Growing teams often include internal staff, contractors, and stakeholders with different levels of access needs.

How to scale it:

- Design **user groups and roles** with tiered permissions in both Jira and Confluence.
- Use **global permissions** in Confluence and **permission schemes** in Jira to control access centrally.
- Consider third-party apps (e.g., *Permission Manager*) for fine-grained control and reporting.

Benefit:

Protects sensitive data and reduces administrative overhead as users scale.

---

3. Use Naming Conventions and Labels for Navigation

As Confluence pages and Jira issues multiply, finding the right content quickly becomes critical.

How to scale it:

- Establish and enforce naming conventions for spaces, pages, and Jira projects.
- Use **consistent page labels** and **issue tags** to aid in filtering and reporting.
- Train teams to use **structured page hierarchies** in Confluence.

Benefit:

Improves navigation, searching, and reporting across large knowledge bases.

---

4. Optimize Performance and System Health

More users and projects can slow down your system if not managed proactively.

How to scale it:

- Regularly archive inactive Jira projects and Confluence spaces.
- Monitor system metrics (e.g., indexing time, load time) via Jira's and Confluence's admin consoles.
- Use **read-only space mode** for legacy Confluence documentation.
- Implement **issue archiving and retention policies**.

Benefit:

Maintains system responsiveness and avoids data bloat.

---

5. Automate Scalable Processes

Manual work doesn't scale. Growth demands automation to maintain speed and accuracy.

How to scale it:

- Use **Jira Automation** to trigger actions based on issue updates, status changes, or field values.
- In Confluence, automate content creation using **page templates with dynamic variables**.
- Consider enterprise automation platforms like **ScriptRunner, Automation for Jira**, or **Power Scripts** for advanced needs.

Benefit:

Reduces errors and frees up your teams to focus on value-driven work.

---

6. Foster a Scalable Integration Culture

Technology alone doesn't scale—people do. A growing organization must embed best practices into its culture.

How to scale it:

- Create **internal Jira-Confluence champions** or "power users" to support local teams.
- Offer regular onboarding and training programs.
- Maintain a central "Integration Best Practices" hub in Confluence.
- Celebrate examples of teams using the tools effectively.

Benefit:

Promotes consistent, scalable adoption across departments and geographies.

Summary

Scaling your Jira and Confluence integration requires more than adding users or licenses. It demands a **strategic approach** to structure, permissions, automation, and culture. With the right foundations in place, your organization can continue growing confidently—without sacrificing the visibility, collaboration, or agility that Jira and Confluence were chosen to deliver.

Adapting to New Jira and Confluence Updates

Staying Future-Ready in a Rapidly Evolving Ecosystem

Jira and Confluence are dynamic platforms that Atlassian consistently enhances through new features, UI changes, and integrations. While these updates aim to improve user experience and platform capabilities, they can also disrupt workflows if organizations are unprepared. For growing teams and enterprises relying on seamless Jira-Confluence integration, **adaptability** is key to maintaining momentum and minimizing disruptions.

This chapter guides you through best practices for staying ahead of updates—so your integration remains robust, secure, and scalable.

The Nature of Atlassian Updates

Atlassian follows a **continuous delivery model**, especially for cloud products, meaning:

- New features roll out frequently
- Deprecated features may be phased out with limited notice
- Admin controls and APIs evolve rapidly
- Marketplace apps must stay in sync with platform changes

Self-hosted (Data Center) users may experience more controlled rollouts, but still face eventual changes during upgrade cycles.

1. Monitor the Atlassian Roadmap and Release Notes

Keeping track of what's coming—and what's just been released—is critical.

How to stay informed:

- Subscribe to Atlassian's [Cloud Roadmap] (https://www.atlassian.com/roadmap/cloud)
- Follow [release blogs] (https://community.atlassian.com/) and [developer changelogs] (https://developer.atlassian.com/changelog)
- Join the Atlassian Community for early discussions about feature rollouts
- Designate an internal Jira-Confluence admin to review weekly update summaries

Benefit:

You'll gain visibility into feature deprecations, breaking changes, and opportunities to improve workflows with new tools.

2. Establish a Sandbox Environment

Never test changes in production. A separate testing environment allows you to validate updates safely.

Setup tips:

- Use Atlassian's free **sandbox feature** (for Premium/Enterprise cloud plans)
- Mirror your key workflows, automation rules, and permission schemes
- Schedule regular "test and verify" sessions after major updates

- In Data Center environments, maintain a staging instance with upgrade mirrors

Benefit:

Reduces risk of breaking integrations, disrupting users, or losing critical data.

---

3. Evaluate Marketplace App Compatibility

When Jira or Confluence updates, apps often lag behind—or introduce their own changes.

What to do:

- Audit which Marketplace apps are mission-critical
- Check version compatibility before upgrading Jira/Confluence
- Subscribe to updates from key vendors
- Limit use of deprecated or poorly maintained plugins

Benefit:

Ensures that integrations and custom enhancements don't become liabilities.

---

4. Adapt Your Workflows to Leverage New Features

Many updates can help your team work smarter—if you adapt your processes.

Examples:

- **Smart Links** and **Inline issue creation** from Confluence
- **Form automation** in Jira Service Management
- **Updated automation builders** for complex rule chaining
- **New macros or page layouts** in Confluence for better visualization

Tip:

Set a quarterly review cadence to identify features that can streamline collaboration or reporting.

---

5. Document Integration Dependencies

When updates hit, knowing what's connected to what is critical.

Create a **Confluence-based integration map** that includes:

- Linked apps and services
- Automation rules and their triggers
- Custom scripts or APIs
- Permission dependencies between Jira and Confluence

Benefit:

Simplifies troubleshooting and speeds up your update readiness assessment.

---

6. Train Your Users Proactively

A feature change that seems minor can confuse users and reduce adoption.

How to stay user-ready:

- Maintain a "What's New in Jira & Confluence" space
- Host short update walkthroughs or demos for team leads
- Create visual guides when UI or feature behaviors change
- Empower team champions to answer questions post-update

Benefit:

Maximizes ROI on new features while minimizing frustration and resistance.

Summary

Jira and Confluence will continue to evolve—fast. But with a proactive strategy, you can **turn change into competitive advantage**. Monitoring updates, testing safely, maintaining compatibility, and empowering your users ensures that your integration remains not only intact, but increasingly powerful.

Preparing for AI-Driven Collaboration Tools

Embracing the Next Frontier in Integrated Project Management

As artificial intelligence (AI) becomes increasingly embedded in enterprise software, tools like Jira and Confluence are beginning to leverage AI-driven features to streamline collaboration, automate mundane tasks, and surface valuable insights. For organizations seeking long-term success with Jira-Confluence integration, preparing for AI adoption is not just optional—it's essential.

This chapter explores the emerging role of AI in project collaboration, what teams can expect from future updates, and how to strategically prepare for AI-powered functionality within the Atlassian ecosystem.

Understanding AI in the Context of Jira and Confluence

AI in project management doesn't mean replacing human decision-makers—it means **augmenting team capabilities** with intelligent assistance. Atlassian's evolving suite of AI features focuses on three core areas:

- **Automation:** Streamlining workflows with smart triggers, conditions, and actions
- **Predictive Insights:** Identifying bottlenecks or risks before they escalate
- **Content Intelligence:** Enhancing documentation, search, and knowledge retrieval

Examples of AI-driven features:

- Jira Smart Suggestions for issue assignees, priorities, or labels
- Confluence Smart Links and inline page summaries
- Predictive issue assignment based on historical patterns
- Natural language querying for issue search and reporting

---

1. Establish a Culture of Automation Readiness

AI thrives in environments that already embrace automation. Begin by encouraging teams to automate:

- Task assignments
- Status transitions
- Notifications and alerts
- Standard documentation templates in Confluence

Then, evaluate where AI could **replace rule-based logic** with **dynamic decision-making** (e.g., smart routing of support tickets or real-time flagging of sprint risks).

Tip:

Audit your current manual processes—AI is most effective where repetitive decisions are made.

---

2. Train Your Team to Trust (and Validate) AI Suggestions

Adoption depends on trust. Teams must understand that AI tools are **assistive**, not authoritative.

Best practices:

- Start with "recommendation-only" AI features that require human approval
- Encourage team retrospectives to review AI-assisted decisions
- Establish feedback loops (thumbs-up/down) for AI output to improve models over time

Example:

In Confluence, when AI generates a page summary, encourage editors to review and refine it rather than discard it.

---

3. Prepare Your Data for AI Consumption

AI models rely heavily on **structured, consistent data**. Disorganized Jira issues or vague Confluence pages hinder accuracy.

Action steps:

- Standardize naming conventions for projects, issues, and labels
- Use structured fields and defined workflows wherever possible
- Organize Confluence spaces and pages with metadata and templates
- Avoid storing key information in unstructured comment threads

Benefit:

Clean data ensures AI can analyze and act more effectively, reducing false positives or irrelevant suggestions.

---

4. Anticipate Privacy and Ethical Considerations

AI capabilities often process sensitive user data, making **privacy and transparency** critical.

Recommendations:

- Review Atlassian's AI privacy policies and opt-in options for new features
- Document how AI is used within your workflows (especially for HR, finance, or client-related projects)
- Consider a data governance policy to handle AI-generated content and decision support

---

5. Invest in AI-Enhanced Marketplace Apps

Many third-party vendors already offer AI-augmented solutions for Jira and Confluence.

Popular examples:

- **Predictive Time Tracking**: Estimates task durations using historical data
- **AI-Powered Knowledge Assistants**: Help users find relevant documents faster in Confluence
- **AI Sprint Analysis**: Identifies risk indicators in agile workflows

Strategy:

Pilot a small set of AI apps and evaluate their ROI before wide rollout.

---

6. Stay Informed and Proactively Upgrade

Atlassian continues to expand its AI initiatives. Upcoming innovations may include:

- **Generative AI** for writing user stories or documentation drafts
- **AI-powered retrospectives** analyzing team dynamics and sprint performance
- **Chat-based assistants** integrated with Jira or Confluence for quick actions

Stay ahead by:

- Joining Atlassian's early access programs or beta testing AI features
- Participating in AI-centric forums or community groups
- Assigning an "AI Champion" within your team to explore and advocate for new capabilities

---

Summary

AI will not replace your project team—but it will **empower them to work smarter, faster, and more strategically**. By embracing automation, ensuring clean data, addressing ethical use, and gradually integrating AI-driven tools, your organization can confidently navigate the next evolution in project collaboration.

The Future of Integrated Project Management

Embracing a Unified, Intelligent, and Adaptive Collaboration Ecosystem

As technology, teams, and workflows continue to evolve, so too must the tools and strategies that power project management. The integration of Jira and Confluence is more than a tactical alignment—it represents a foundational shift toward **seamless collaboration, transparency, and operational agility**.

In this closing chapter, we look ahead at the trends, technologies, and practices that will define the **next era of integrated project management**, helping your organization stay competitive, innovative, and future-ready.

---

1. Intelligent Collaboration Will Be the New Standard

The future will not be about simply linking tools—it will be about enabling **intelligent synergy** between them. Platforms like Jira and Confluence will increasingly leverage:

- **AI-driven decision support** for planning, prioritization, and risk detection
- **Context-aware content recommendations** in Confluence based on Jira activity
- **Smart notifications** that adapt to user behavior and work patterns
- **Predictive analytics** to anticipate blockers or capacity issues

Impact:

Teams will spend less time managing tools and more time focused on value-adding activities, with intelligent automation handling repetitive processes.

---

2. Real-Time, Multi-Modal Collaboration

Project collaboration will expand beyond pages and tickets. Expect to see:

- **Integrated whiteboards and visual planning spaces** embedded in Jira/Confluence
- **Live co-editing** on Confluence documents with contextual Jira updates
- **Voice- and video-enhanced workflows**, such as AI-transcribed meetings linked to Jira epics
- **Asynchronous collaboration tools** that adapt to distributed and hybrid teams

Tip:

Prepare your teams by training them in new modes of collaboration that go beyond traditional documentation or status updates.

---

3. Hyper-Customization with Modular Platforms

Rather than using "out-of-the-box" configurations, future teams will demand **modular, low-code interfaces** tailored to their specific workflows.

You'll see:

- **Custom dashboards** combining Jira, Confluence, and other tools
- **Drag-and-drop workflow builders** that define logic across platforms
- **Role-specific views** with personalized data summaries and action prompts

- **Marketplace apps** evolving into microservices that plug into a unified collaboration layer

Strategy:

Invest in admin training or internal champions who can configure and optimize modular setups.

---

4. Data Unification and Integration Beyond Atlassian

In the future, Jira and Confluence will not operate in isolation but as **hubs** within a larger tech ecosystem. Integration with CRMs, HR tools, analytics platforms, and developer pipelines will become routine.

Key trends:

- **API-first architectures** enabling deep customization
- **Data lakes and unified reporting layers** to analyze performance across platforms
- **Federated search** across Jira, Confluence, Slack, Google Drive, etc.
- **Unified authentication and access control** using SSO and identity providers

Recommendation:

Map your organization's tech stack and explore how Jira-Confluence integration can bridge more systems for end-to-end visibility.

---

5. Evolving Roles and Responsibilities

As tools get smarter, team dynamics will shift:

- **Project managers** will act more as facilitators of flow and culture
- **Engineers and creators** will increasingly rely on collaborative automation
- **Cross-functional roles** will emerge, blending technical and strategic collaboration skillsets
- **AI trainers and governance leaders** may become critical to overseeing ethical, effective tool use

Insight:

Develop cross-disciplinary training programs that empower users to become confident system collaborators—not just task executors.

---

6. Strategic Focus on Resilience and Scalability

Lastly, the future of project management isn't just about being faster—it's about being **more resilient, adaptive, and scalable**.

This means:

- Designing systems that can flex with team size, structure, and global distribution
- Establishing **processes that self-improve** based on analytics and feedback
- Ensuring that knowledge is not siloed but accessible and usable across time zones and departments
- Using **data-driven retrospectives** to evolve best practices continually

---

Final Thoughts

The integration of Jira with Confluence is not the end goal—it's the launchpad for building a **future-ready project ecosystem**. By embracing new technologies, staying open to organizational change, and focusing on user-centric collaboration, your team can thrive in an increasingly complex and dynamic landscape.

The future of integrated project management is unified, intelligent, and human-centric. And it starts now—with you.

Conclusion

Recap: Key Takeaways for Success

Harnessing Integration to Drive Collaborative Excellence

Throughout this book, we have explored the intricate yet powerful synergy between Jira and Confluence—two of the most capable tools in modern project management. Whether you're a team leader, project manager, agile coach, or enterprise architect, the knowledge and strategies outlined in previous chapters aim to empower you to create a more **cohesive, efficient, and intelligent collaboration framework**.

This recap distills the core lessons and best practices to help you retain the most impactful insights and apply them with confidence.

---

1. Understand the Unique Strengths of Jira and Confluence

- **Jira** excels at issue tracking, agile workflow management, and sprint execution.
- **Confluence** is unmatched in collaborative documentation, team knowledge sharing, and real-time planning.
- When integrated, these platforms **eliminate silos** and foster **end-to-end project visibility**.

Key Tip: Leverage Jira for task coordination and Confluence for strategic communication—they are complementary, not overlapping.

---

2. Preparation is Half the Battle

Before diving into integration, ensure that:

- Your **team's needs and expectations** are clearly defined
- **Stakeholders are aligned** on goals and implementation priorities
- The **technical prerequisites** (user access, tool versions, permissions) are in place

Key Tip: A clear roadmap and stakeholder buy-in are critical for a smooth and sustainable rollout.

---

3. Start Simple, Scale Strategically

Begin your integration with high-impact, low-complexity use cases:

- Link Jira issues to Confluence meeting notes or specs
- Embed project boards or filters in relevant pages
- Use macros to create **interactive content** that evolves with your sprints

From there, gradually adopt **automation**, **permissions syncing**, and **custom templates**.

Key Tip: Let real team needs guide your integration depth—avoid forcing features for the sake of completeness.

4. Foster a Culture of Transparency and Collaboration

The tools alone don't make collaboration seamless—**your team habits do**. Integration works best when:

- Confluence is used for **active planning**, not just passive documentation
- Jira becomes a **single source of truth** for task status and blockers
- Meetings, standups, and retrospectives refer to both platforms simultaneously

Key Tip: Encourage cross-functional workflows where every update, document, or task lives in an integrated ecosystem.

5. Explore Advanced Features with Purpose

Once your team is comfortable, enhance your setup with:

- **Custom Jira filters** displayed in Confluence dashboards
- **API integrations** and scripts for automating repetitive updates
- **Marketplace apps** tailored to your industry or workflow
- **Custom workflows** that span Jira tasking and Confluence approvals

Key Tip: Advanced doesn't mean complicated—every enhancement should simplify your team's work.

6. Continuously Measure, Optimize, and Evolve

Your Jira-Confluence integration is not a one-time project—it's an ongoing capability. Build a culture of improvement by:

- Collecting feedback from users
- Monitoring tool performance and data consistency
- Reviewing workflows quarterly for redundancy or gaps
- Keeping up with new features and releases from Atlassian

Key Tip: Make time for regular retrospectives focused on tooling, not just tasks.

Final Words

Seamless collaboration is not just about software—it's about **connecting people, processes, and information**. When implemented with clarity and purpose, Jira and Confluence together offer a robust foundation for:

- Agile transformation
- Scalable enterprise planning
- Unified communication
- Transparent execution

By following the strategies in this book, you are well-equipped to **future-proof your project management framework** and lead your team into a new era of integrated collaboration.

Success is not in the tools—but in how you use them together.

Next Steps for Continuous Improvement

Embracing Iteration in Your Jira-Confluence Journey

Integration is not a finish line—it's a **living, evolving process**. As you wrap up this book, the most important mindset to adopt is one of **continuous improvement**. The value of integrating Jira with Confluence isn't just about initial setup or clever features; it's about how well the system grows **with your team's maturity, needs, and goals**.

This chapter outlines a strategic approach to evolving your integrated framework long after the initial deployment.

---

1. Conduct Regular Tool Audits

Evaluate your Jira and Confluence usage at regular intervals—quarterly or bi-annually.

- Are your custom workflows still relevant?
- Are dashboards, pages, and issue types aligned with your current projects?
- Are there underused features or outdated templates that need retiring?

Action Tip: Create a recurring "tool health check" with key stakeholders and power users.

---

2. Gather and Act on User Feedback

Your end users—developers, PMs, marketers, and designers—are your best feedback source.

- Run short surveys or feedback sessions
- Track common questions and support issues
- Identify friction points in user adoption or interface navigation

Action Tip: Establish a feedback loop with a simple Confluence page to log suggestions and status.

---

3. Stay Updated with New Features

Atlassian regularly rolls out new capabilities, especially AI enhancements, automation improvements, and UI refinements.

- Subscribe to Jira and Confluence release notes
- Join Atlassian community forums or newsletters
- Pilot new features in a sandbox environment before rolling them out

Action Tip: Assign a "Tool Champion" role on your team to monitor updates and propose rollouts.

---

4. Train and Upskill Your Team

Tool maturity is a direct reflection of team capability. Make continuous learning part of your team culture.

- Host internal training sessions or micro-learning workshops
- Share helpful Confluence pages, Loom videos, or tooltips

- Document best practices in a shared "Team Guidebook" space in Confluence

Action Tip: Create onboarding modules tailored to different roles using Jira-Confluence tutorials.

---

5. Expand Your Integration Ecosystem

Once you've mastered core integrations, look beyond Jira and Confluence to build a holistic system.

- Connect with tools like Trello, Slack, Microsoft Teams, Figma, or Bitbucket
- Explore marketplace apps for Gantt charts, custom automations, or resource planning
- Use APIs to create automated bridges with CRM or HR platforms

Action Tip: Map your team's daily tools and identify integration gaps that Jira-Confluence can help close.

---

6. Review KPIs and Project Outcomes

Your system should not only *feel* efficient but also *prove* its value.

- Define measurable outcomes: ticket throughput, sprint velocity, knowledge reuse rate, etc.
- Review team retrospectives for mentions of tools helping or hindering progress
- Adjust workflows, templates, or dashboards based on insights

Action Tip: Use Jira dashboards and Confluence reports to visualize performance over time.

---

7. Plan for Scalability and Resilience

As your team grows or your business scales, your tool architecture must adapt.

- Document current integrations and workflows for easier replication
- Standardize templates and naming conventions
- Invest in data backups, permission audits, and redundancy planning

Action Tip: Treat your integrated system as mission-critical infrastructure, not a side tool.

Final Thought

Continuous improvement is not about perfection—it's about **progress with purpose**. Jira and Confluence, when actively managed, evolve from productivity tools into a **central nervous system** for your projects.

Keep refining. Keep learning. And keep building a collaborative culture that turns **transparency and efficiency** into your team's competitive advantage.

Your journey doesn't end here—it accelerates.

Appendices

Appendix A: Glossary of Key Terms

Agile

A project management methodology focused on iterative development, collaboration, and flexibility. Jira is widely used in Agile teams to manage sprints, backlogs, and issue tracking.

API (Application Programming Interface)

A set of functions and protocols that allow different software applications to communicate with each other. Jira and Confluence provide REST APIs for automation and advanced integrations.

Atlassian

The company behind Jira, Confluence, Bitbucket, and other collaboration tools. Atlassian products are designed to support project management, software development, and team collaboration.

Backlog

A prioritized list of work items, often user stories or tasks, waiting to be addressed in future sprints. Managed within Jira for Agile projects.

Board

A visual interface in Jira used to represent workflows. Common board types include Scrum and Kanban, allowing teams to track progress across different stages.

Confluence

A team workspace and knowledge management platform developed by Atlassian. Used for creating, sharing, and collaborating on content, documentation, and project plans.

Dashboard

A customizable interface in Jira or Confluence used to visualize project metrics, issue statuses, sprint progress, and more.

Epic

A large body of work that can be broken down into smaller tasks or stories. Used in Agile methodology and represented in Jira as a high-level issue type.

Integration

The process of connecting Jira and Confluence (or other tools) to enable seamless data sharing, enhanced workflows, and improved team collaboration.

Issue

A core unit of work in Jira, which can represent a task, bug, story, or epic. Issues are tracked through workflows until completion.

Jira

A project management and issue tracking tool developed by Atlassian, commonly used by software development and Agile teams.

Kanban

A visual workflow management method used to limit work in progress and increase efficiency. Jira supports Kanban boards for continuous delivery teams.

Macro

Reusable components in Confluence that allow dynamic content such as Jira issue filters, tables, charts, and other integrations.

Marketplace

Atlassian's platform for third-party apps and plugins that extend the functionality of Jira and Confluence.

Permission Scheme

A system in Jira or Confluence for managing who can view, edit, comment, or administer specific content or projects.

Project

In Jira, a structured workspace for managing issues, workflows, and reports. Projects can represent teams, products, or initiatives.

Sprint

A fixed time-boxed iteration used in Scrum methodology. Jira enables sprint planning, execution, and retrospective tracking.

Template

Predefined content structures in Confluence or Jira used to maintain consistency. Templates can be customized for meeting notes, product requirements, or issue types.

User Story

A small, self-contained unit of work that represents a user requirement or need. Often written in the format: "As a [user], I want [goal] so that [reason]."

Workflow

The sequence of statuses and transitions an issue moves through during its lifecycle. Jira workflows can be customized to match team processes.

This glossary is intended to help new users and stakeholders develop a clear understanding of key terms used throughout your Jira-Confluence integration journey. Refer back as needed while implementing the concepts in this book.

Appendix B: Recommended Plugins and Extensions

To fully leverage the power of Jira and Confluence integration, numerous plugins and extensions are available on the Atlassian Marketplace. These tools can streamline workflows, enhance collaboration, and add powerful capabilities beyond the native features. Below is a curated list of highly recommended plugins and extensions organized by functionality.

1. Integration and Synchronization

ScriptRunner for Jira & Confluence

- Adds powerful automation and scripting capabilities.
- Enables custom scripts for workflows, issue transitions, and content generation.
- Essential for advanced users managing large, complex environments.

Elements Connect

- Integrates external data sources (like databases or CRMs) directly into Jira fields.
- Useful for keeping Jira issues synced with outside systems.

Backbone Issue Sync

- Enables cross-project and cross-instance Jira synchronization.
- Ideal for enterprises working across departments or with external partners.

2. Reporting and Dashboards

eazyBI Reports and Charts

- Advanced data visualization and reporting tool.
- Supports Jira issue analysis, sprint reports, and Confluence dashboard embedding.

Rich Filters for Jira Dashboards

- Enhances Jira dashboards with clickable filters, dynamic charts, and multiple views.

Table Filter and Charts for Confluence

- Adds advanced table filtering, pivot tables, and visualizations within Confluence pages.

3. Document and Content Management

Scroll Versions

- Version control for Confluence pages.
- Enables publishing documentation based on product versions, great for software teams.

Comala Document Management

- Adds workflows, approvals, and document states in Confluence.

- Perfect for regulated industries or teams needing structured documentation processes.

Advanced Tables for Confluence

- Offers improved control over table formatting and appearance in Confluence.

---

4. Agile and DevOps Enhancements

BigPicture

- Project portfolio management plugin with Gantt charts, roadmaps, and risk matrices.
- Integrates closely with both Jira and Confluence.

Structure – Project Management at Scale

- Provides a hierarchy builder for organizing Jira issues into trees.
- Great for planning large-scale projects with dependencies.

Automation for Jira (Built-in but enhanced with Pro features)

- Enables powerful "if-then" rules without scripting.
- Automates repetitive tasks like issue transitions or email notifications.

---

5. Collaboration and Productivity

Team Calendars for Confluence

- Adds shared team calendars to Confluence for tracking sprints, leaves, and releases.

Gliffy Diagrams / Draw.io for Confluence

- Diagram tools to visualize workflows, architectures, and team processes.
- Useful for documenting project logic or visual planning.

Content Formatting Macros for Confluence

- Provides additional UI elements (tabs, buttons, panels) to enrich Confluence pages.

---

6. Security and Permissions

Permission Schemes Auditor for Jira

- Helps visualize and audit permission schemes.
- Useful during user role restructuring or onboarding new teams.

Space Admin for Confluence

- Empowers space administrators to manage permissions and content more effectively.

Final Tip

When selecting plugins:

- **Start with your team's biggest bottlenecks.** Choose tools that solve current pain points.
- **Avoid plugin overload.** Each plugin introduces overhead—stick to essentials.
- **Test in staging environments.** Especially critical for large-scale integrations.

All plugins mentioned are available through the [Atlassian Marketplace] (https://marketplace.atlassian.com/). Be sure to check compatibility with your Jira and Confluence versions before installation.

Appendix C: Further Reading and Resources

To help you deepen your knowledge and stay current with the evolving capabilities of Jira, Confluence, and integrated project management strategies, this appendix provides a curated list of authoritative resources. These include official documentation, expert blogs, relevant books, and active community hubs that offer practical insights, tutorials, and updates.

1. Official Documentation and Learning Platforms

Atlassian Documentation

- [Jira Software Documentation] (https://support.atlassian.com/jira-software-cloud/)
- [Confluence Documentation] (https://support.atlassian.com/confluence-cloud/)
- These are your go-to references for configuration, features, and troubleshooting.

Atlassian University

- [university.atlassian.com] (https://university.atlassian.com)
- Offers free and paid courses on Jira and Confluence. Includes certifications and role-based learning paths (Admin, User, Project Manager).

2. Books for Deeper Insight

"Jira Strategy Admin Workbook" by Rachel Wright

- A practical guide for Jira administrators with templates, best practices, and scalable configuration strategies.

"Confluence, Tech Comm, and Chocolate" by Sarah Maddox

- Explores how to use Confluence for technical communication, team collaboration, and project documentation.

"Effective Project Management with Jira" by Patrick Li

- Covers how to manage agile and non-agile projects using Jira, including workflows and reporting strategies.

3. Community Forums and User Groups

Atlassian Community

- [community.atlassian.com] (https://community.atlassian.com)
- Active forums where you can ask questions, find answers, and connect with Jira and Confluence users around the world.

LinkedIn Groups

- *Jira & Confluence Administrators* and *Atlassian Users Worldwide*
- Good places for professional networking and tip-sharing.

Meetup.com – Atlassian User Groups (AUGs)

- Local meetups and virtual events hosted by Atlassian to connect users and share case studies, solutions, and product updates.

---

4. Blogs and Expert Sources

Atlassian Blog

- [blog.atlassian.com] (https://blog.atlassian.com)
- Regular articles on feature releases, product integrations, team productivity, and innovation.

Adaptavist Blog

- [www.adaptavist.com/blog] (https://www.adaptavist.com/blog)
- Covers advanced use cases, scripting, and enterprise-level Jira/Confluence solutions.

Communardo Blog

- [www.communardo.com/blog] (https://www.communardo.com/blog)
- Offers insights into Confluence collaboration strategies and plugin integrations.

---

5. Useful Tools and Resources

Jira Plugin Compatibility Checker

- [marketplace.atlassian.com] (https://marketplace.atlassian.com)
- Helps confirm which plugins work with your current Jira/Confluence versions.

Draw.io for Confluence

- [www.draw.io] (https://www.draw.io)
- A powerful diagramming tool used widely in Confluence pages for architecture, workflows, and planning visuals.

REST API References

- [Jira REST API] (https://developer.atlassian.com/cloud/jira/platform/rest/v3/)
- [Confluence REST API] (https://developer.atlassian.com/cloud/confluence/rest/)
- Essential for automating tasks and building custom integrations.

Bookmark these resources and revisit them regularly. As Atlassian's products evolve, staying informed is key to maintaining an efficient, secure, and collaborative project management environment.

Printed in Dunstable, United Kingdom